AMERICAN AUTOBIOGRAPHY

T0386798

BAAS Paperbacks

www.euppublishing.com/series/baas

American Autobiography

RACHAEL MCLENNAN

EDINBURGH
University Press

© Rachael McLennan, 2013

Edinburgh University Press Ltd
22 George Square, Edinburgh

Typeset in Fournier by
Koinonia, Manchester, and
printed and bound in Great Britain by
CPI Group (UK) Ltd, Croydon CRO 4YY

A CIP Record for this book is available from the British Library

ISBN 978 0 7486 4461 2 (hardback)
ISBN 978 0 7486 4460 5 (paperback)
ISBN 978 0 7486 4462 9 (webready PDF)
ISBN 978 0 7486 7046 8 (epub)
ISBN 978 0 7486 7045 1 (Amazon ebook)

Published with the support of the Edinburgh University
Scholarly Publishing Initiatives Fund.

Contents

Acknowledgements

That this textbook exists is due, in large part, to Simon Newman, who first suggested to me that I should write it. I thank him for this and for the invaluable support that he and Carol Smith have given to this project, in their roles as series editors. Grateful acknowledgement is also made to the readers of my book proposal, who made useful suggestions about how it might be developed.

While working on this project, I was encouraged in a great variety of ways by my colleagues in the School of American Studies at the University of East Anglia. Particular thanks must go to Sarah Garland, with whom I had a number of conversations which proved vital to my thinking in these pages, and to the students I taught in my American Autobiography module, who also helped me clarify points and determine how this textbook could be most useful.

This book is dedicated to my family.

Introduction:
American Autobiography

Jonathan Franzen's *Freedom* (2010) explores the long, difficult marriage of an American couple, Patty and Walter Berglund. The novel tells the story of how Patty and Walter meet and start a family. It relates the breakdown of their relationship and its eventual repair in the years of the early twenty-first century. It raises questions about how the Berglunds (separately and together) participate in, and are constructed by, mythologies and ideologies pertaining to the concept of 'freedom' in American culture from the mid-twentieth to the twenty-first century and how this may have contributed to the failure (or success) of their union. Narrated, for the most part, in the omniscient third-person, using free indirect discourse to present numerous characters intimately (such as Walter, the Berglunds' son, Joey, family 'friend' Richard Katz), it is nonetheless Patty who receives particular attention and scrutiny – so much so, that two of the novel's five sections comprise her autobiographical narratives. The second section is entitled 'MISTAKES WERE MADE Autobiography of Patty Berglund by Patty Berglund (Composed at Her Therapist's Suggestion)', while the fourth, penultimate section is entitled 'MISTAKES WERE MADE (CONCLUSION) A Sort of Letter to Her Reader by Patty Berglund'. These sections, however, are also largely narrated in the third person. They seem addressed to Walter, in particular. To compound confusion, the sections are interspersed with comic, and frequently disconcerting, commentaries, which function to remind readers of their 'autobiographical' status. For example, following her separation from Walter and the death of Lalitha – a woman with whom Walter begins a brief relationship – Patty's 'sort of letter to her reader' begins as follows:

> The autobiographer, mindful of her reader and the loss he suffered, and mindful that a certain kind of voice would do well to fall silent in

the face of life's increasing somberness, has been trying very hard to write these pages in first and second person. But she seems doomed, alas, as a writer, to be one of those jocks who refer to themselves in third person. Although she believes herself to be genuinely changed, and doing infinitely better than in the old days, and therefore worthy of a fresh hearing, she still can't bring herself to let go of a voice she found when she had nothing else to hold on to, even if it means that her reader throws this document straight into his old Macalester College wastebasket. (Franzen 2010: 507)

Patty's surmise that Walter may throw her second autobiographical narrative out seems well-founded; after all, the first autobiographical narrative directly caused the definitive break in their relationship. This break occurs when Katz, with whom Patty has cheated on Walter, visits the Berglunds' home. He enters the bedroom, where he intends to spend the night. Fantasising that he might find Patty on the bed, he finds, instead, her 'Autobiography'. First, he reads it:

He noted how much more interested he was in the pages about himself than in the other pages; it confirmed his long-standing suspicion that people ultimately only want to read about themselves. He noted further, with pleasure, that this self of his had genuinely fascinated Patty; it reminded him of why he liked her. (Franzen 2010: 377)

Katz is chastened to discover that 'the document had obviously been written for Walter, as a kind of heartsick undeliverable apology to him' (Franzen 2010: 377). In a gesture prompted by decidedly mixed motives, both spiteful and generous, he leaves the autobiography on the desk in Walter's office as he exits the Berglunds' home – a 'little parting gift' (Franzen 2010: 378). Katz believes that Patty wants him to give the document to Walter:

Somebody had to clear the air around here, somebody had to put an end to the bullshit, and Patty obviously wasn't up to it. And so she wanted Katz to do the dirty work? Well, fine. [...] His job in life was to speak the dirty truth. (Franzen 2010: 378)

Initially, Katz's gesture has only negative consequences. It is by reading the autobiography that Walter learns about the affair. This discovery results in Patty leaving the family home (and, briefly, taking up residence with Katz). In the longer term, though, the long, bitter chain of events set in motion by Katz's act of giving the autobiography to Walter results in reconciliation. And it is Katz who suggests to Patty, after her separation from Walter, that she write the second autobiographical narrative: "'You know how to tell a story," [Katz] said. "Why don't you tell him a story?"' (Franzen 2010: 537). It is never confirmed that Walter reads the whole of that 'story', Patty's 'sort of letter to her reader', but reading only 'one short paragraph' of it (2010: 557) (in all probability, the passage quoted above) prompts him to run to his doorstep, outside which Patty is waiting stubbornly, in the freezing cold:

> 'I don't want this!' he shouted at her. 'I don't want to read you! I want you to take this and get in your car and warm up, because it's fucking freezing out here.' (Franzen 2010: 557)

Despite Walter's anger and refusals to read, or to engage with, Patty – 'He came from a long line of refusers, he had the constitution for it' (Franzen 2010: 555) – connection has been made and is desired. So the novel comes to its end, and so begins the resumption of the Berglunds' imperfect relationship.

It may seem peculiar to introduce a textbook on American autobiography with discussion of an autobiography which exists within a fiction and which is, therefore (and it is imperative to remember this), *not* autobiography. But is it peculiar? Consideration of the role of autobiography in Franzen's novel reveals many issues which are crucial to the study of this fascinating topic. This will, hopefully, become apparent over the course of this introduction and throughout this volume. And it must be confessed that autobiography, whatever it is (and just what autobiography is, is a vexed and vexing question), is peculiar. Autobiography is extremely difficult to describe and define. Eve Sedgwick's description of the effects of the word 'queer' is also applicable to autobiography:

> Queer is a continuing moment, movement, motive – recurrent, eddying, *troublant*. The word 'queer' itself means *across* – it comes from the Indo-European root -*twerkw*, which also yields the German *quer* (transverse), Latin *torquere* (to twist), English *athwart*. [...] The immemorial current that *queer* represents is antiseparatist [sic] as it is antiassimilationist [sic]. Keenly, it is relational, and strange. (1994: viii)

'Troublant', 'relational', 'strange' – these words are essential. In discussions about defining autobiography, Philippe Lejeune's claim that autobiography is a 'retrospective prose narrative written by a real person concerning his own existence, where the focus is his individual life, in particular the story of his personality' is often cited (Lejeune, in Eakin 1989: 4, emphasis in original). But more often than not, Lejeune's definition is acknowledged only to be refused, for the purposes of noting all the ways it is inadequate. This strange, critical gesture stands as just one example of the difficulties of definition. Linda Anderson notes that:

> The very pervasiveness and slipperiness of autobiography has made the need to contain and control it within disciplinary boundaries all the more urgent, and many literary critics have turned to definitions as a way of stamping their authority on an unruly and even slightly disreputable field. (2011: 1–2)

Certainly, there is much to fault in Lejeune's definition. Must an autobiography be retrospective? The format of a diary, for example, complicates this. Must an autobiography be written in prose? The poetic examples of autobiography discussed in this study, by Walt Whitman and Lyn Hejinian, indicate that it need not. Who determines who is a 'person'? Let alone a 'real' person? Identity and authority are inextricably involved in the production and reception of any autobiography, while the question of the 'real' alludes to the problems of reference which autobiography poses.

Specific ideologies of identity and authority are present in Lejeune's definition. What of the insistence on male pronouns? Reading Lejeune's definition literally would lead to the conclusion that Patty would never be capable of producing autobiography, because of her gender. Does autobiography really only focus on an individual life? The importance of Walter to Patty's narratives, as their addressee (his reactions to her autobiographical writings are vitally significant) and as a personage described within their pages – one who is influential in determining the course of Patty's life – would suggest that this is absolutely not the case. Lejeune's privileging of the individual, though, reflects the Western privileging of individualism and, with that, a model of identity as isolated, independent, self-determining (one which, as Lejeune's work indicates, has generally been figured male). This privileging of individualism suggests that one important factor on which the production and reception of any autobiography has depended (especially an American autobiography, perhaps) is whether it is written by an individual who participates in – or feels excluded from – a culture which prizes individualism.

Must an autobiography describe 'the story of personality'? This raises the questions of generic classification that autobiography poses – is that 'story' a history? A fiction? Both? Neither? Intriguingly, different English translations of Lejeune's essay alter the terms of the definition: for example, one translation cites 'in particular on *the development of* his personality' (Lejeune, in Todorov 1977: 193), rather than '*the story of* personality' (my emphases). A focus on 'development' alludes to central concerns of autobiography – examination and explanation of how identity is understood, formed, narrated. In many ways, Patty's autobiographical narratives focus on 'the development of personality'. They often take the form of self-defence or apology (mistakes were made), with her 'personality' offered as explanation (or excuse) for her behaviour.

It is helpful to think of autobiography as comprising an explanation of the self – how the self came to be, why the autobiographer is as he or she is at the time of writing. Autobiographers want to explain why they have written, and why readers should read, their autobiographies. Often they want to explain what they understand to be the meaning and purpose of autobiography. Here, for example, is Barack Obama's attempt to accomplish exactly these aims, in the preface to the first edition of his autobiography, *Dreams From My Father*, in 1995:

> At some point, then, in spite of a stubborn desire to protect myself from scrutiny, in spite of the periodic impulse to abandon the entire project, what has found its way onto these pages is a record of a personal, interior journey – a boy's search for his father, and through that a search a workable meaning for his life as a black American. The result is autobiographical, although whenever someone's asked me over the course of the last three years just what the book is about, I've usually avoided such a description. An autobiography promises feats worthy of record, conversations with famous people, a central role in important events. There is none of that here. At the very least, an autobiography implies a summing up, a certain closure, that hardly suits someone of my years, still busy charting his way through the world. ([2004] 2007: xvi)

In a gesture which echoes the manner in which many critics deal with Lejeune's description, Obama explains how he understands autobiography, only for the purpose of refusing to locate his own text comfortably within the description he offers. Not all autobiographies describe the development of personality and certainly not necessarily in the orderly, coherent sense that Lejeune's definition (or the translation of the definition) may imply; Obama refuses closure. For Obama, as for many autobiographers, producing autobiography has been perilous – the project was often attended by doubts regarding the possibility of its completion. Patty's speculation that Walter may throw her autobiography in the 'wastebasket' also indicates her awareness of the fragile existence of her text.

As thoroughly unsatisfactory as Lejeune's definition is, then, it is useful, because it illustrates the important fact that finding a workable definition of autobiography is no simple task. His definition is useful, because it is inadequate; it provokes the vital questions asked above. It is because it does so, that his definition is usually cited (offered), then refused. All of the questions Lejeune's definition raises pertain to the tripartite structure of the word 'autobiography' itself. Sidonie Smith and Julia Watson note that the word derives from the Greek *autos* (self), *bios* (life) and *graphe* (writing) (2010: 1). The arguments about autobiography made in this textbook take the form of refusals of many sorts, and a resistance to understanding autobiography as the sum of these three parts (self, life, writing) constitutes one important refusal. Understanding autobiography as the sum of those three parts suggests that the problem of defining autobiography can be resolved – that there is a last word to be said on the subject. Rather – and this is one of the central contentions made in this study – autobiography should be understood as comprising the *relations* between those parts, relations which are different in every autobiography. Henry Adams, whose autobiography will be discussed in this volume, describes himself as a historian involved in 'the study of relation' (2008: 8); autobiographies are studies of many kinds of relations. As such, they prompt yet more difficult questions: What is identity? How to write one's life – truthfully? Why write one's life? How might writing the life affect the life (for good or ill)? Whose life does an autobiography affect – only the writer's? Or those of others?

This study also contends that autobiography is often rendered difficult and dangerous, because so many writers and readers of autobiography confuse the three parts (self, life, writing). Confusion, defined in the Oxford English Dictionary as involving 'discomfiture, overthrow, ruin, destruction, perdition', is a central, affective response in the writing, reading and critical study of autobiographies. The dictionary definition also suggests that confusion involves a 'putting to shame' – another affect shared by autobiographers and readers (for any number of reasons, autobiographers are often ashamed about making a private history public, and autobiographies often deliberately aim to induce shame in their readers). This confusion can be productive. For example, it reveals how difficult it is to separate, or distinguish between, the self, the life and the writing. Katz hopes to find Patty on his bed, but her autobiography is there, instead. Angrily, Walter tells Patty: "'I don't want to read you!'", confusing her text for her person. Walter's confusion of autobiography and the self – which Amy Hungerford might call the 'personification of the text' (2003) – is one of the most commonly made, and most dangerous, confusions. It is ethically problematic: what does it mean to attribute the qualities of a person to a text? What does it mean to consider autobiography as if it is a living thing? Confusions in distinguishing between self, life and writing often involve (or are prompted by) various kinds of substitution, as Katz's and Walter's do. These substitutions are often metonymic (metonymy is another important feature of autobiography). They also involve displacements (autobiography is often described as taking writer and reader on a journey of self-discovery). Readers must examine the complex confusions which are enacted in specific autobiographical texts.

Obama's refusal to locate himself within his understanding of autobiography takes the form of breaking a 'promise' he believes autobiography makes, with regard to what it will offer: 'feats worthy of record, conversations with famous people, a central role in important events'. That 'promise' is founded on characteristics which have, historically, defined a particular kind of autobiography – the memoir, a record of a subject (usually white, male, a public figure). Indeed, one confusion surrounding autobiography relates to another kind of substitution: the frequent interchangeability of the terms 'memoir' and 'autobiography', an understanding of them as synonyms, despite the fact that biographies can be considered 'memoir', too. [1] Some readers deal with this confusion by introducing the term 'life writing', which currently receives sustained critical attention. Autobiography is an example of life writing, a particular kind of life narrative.

While 'memoir' has been understood as a subgenre of autobiography and biography (Couser 2012: 17–18), 'life writing' also insufficiently marks the distinctiveness of autobiographical writing (the self writes about itself). In this textbook, I privilege the term 'autobiography', because of a sense that it does describe a particular kind of life writing, but can apply to a wide range of texts. I also dispute Couser's contention that '"memoir" has eclipsed "autobiography" as the term of choice for a certain kind of life narrative' (2012: 3). Indeed, Smith and Watson note that despite challenges to the term 'autobiography', because of ways in which the term may (too narrowly) designate a certain kind of writing subject, 'autobiography' 'remains the widely used and most generally understood term' (2010: 2–3). However, it must also be noted that works first referred to as autobiography were those produced at 'a particular historical juncture, the period prior to the Enlightenment in the West. Central to that movement was the concept of the self-interested individual of property who was intent on assessing the status of the sound or the meaning of public achievement' (2010: 2). That Obama's text breaks the 'promise' of autobiography, therefore, signals that his text, like many others, refuses to conform to those values and ideologies; indeed, this is why some writers and critics are uncomfortable with the term 'autobiography'. Obama's autobiography engages in a political act of refusing the privileging of the white, male subject, whose identity, privileges and narratives are thoroughly embedded within, and valorised throughout, much of the history of autobiography. A focus on the term 'autobiography' to describe the (very different) texts discussed in this volume functions to emphasise (but not privilege) the Enlightenment ideologies of identity which produced the white, male, public subject that autobiography's early examples so often represent. These ideologies constitute a significant legacy for the production and study of autobiography today. And it also emphasises the fact that the relationship of many autobiographies to that Enlightenment legacy has been, and still is, one of discomfiture and confusion.

Another central contention made in this study is that the relationship between autobiography and another kind of promise – what Lauren Berlant calls America's 'national promise' of the realisation of 'abstract principles of democratic nationality' (1997: 18–19) – is central to understanding American autobiography and ensures that many American autobiographies have political and ethical designs (Franzen's novel explores one of these abstract principles – freedom). All the texts discussed in the following chapters are marked by a relationship to that promise, although they enact that relationship very differently. Obama refuses that national promise, but he also 'renews' it (interestingly, the subtitle of a collection of his speeches published in 2008 claims exactly this). In his 'A More Perfect Union' speech, Obama describes himself as follows:

I am the son of a black man from Kenya and a white woman from Kansas. I was raised with the help of a white grandfather who survived a Depression to serve in Patton's Army during World War II and a white grandmother who worked on a bomber assembly line at Fort Leavenworth while he was overseas. I've gone to some of the best schools in America and lived in one of the world's poorest nations. I am married to a black American who carries within her the blood of slaves and slaveowners – an inheritance we pass on to our two precious daughters. I have brothers, sisters, nieces, nephews, uncles and cousins, of every race and every hue scattered across three continents, and for as long as I live, I will never forget that in no other country on Earth is my story even possible.

It's a story that hasn't made me the most conventional candidate. But it is a story that has seared into my genetic makeup the idea that this nation is more than the sum of its parts – that out of many, we are truly one. (2008: 227)

Obama's attitude, here, is displayed in *Dreams From My Father*, which, Georgiana Banita argues, exemplifies a model of 'transnational self-reliance' (Banita 2010). Obama inscribes himself as a transnational subject, but in ways which, he argues, are (and could only be) distinctively American (is there an uncomfortable confusion of 'American' and 'transnational' here?). Banita argues that Obama's self-reliance functions 'not in opposition to the transnational scope of his writings, but as a key to his vision of American exceptionalism in a newly globalised world' (2010: 26). That is, Obama foregrounds himself as a transnational subject, not in order to dispense with the national promise, only to expand the scope of its bounds, and to claim that his life history demonstrates how the promise has been kept. The presence of American exceptionalism in his account may be troubling, as this ideology has placed (and still places) limitations on the autobiographies which are valued in American culture and the subjects who have been described (or can describe themselves) as 'American'. In many autobiographies examined in this textbook, the 'national promise' is not regarded with Obama's confidence and optimism and is understood, instead, in terms of failure: autobiographers describe how there has been a failure to keep, or realise, the promise. These descriptions often take the form of refusals, and this study argues that the gesture of refusal is central to the aims and reception of many American autobiographies (it is stressed that Walter comes from a 'long line of refusers' – it is in his 'constitution'). It is because ideologies of American exceptionalism have also limited the critical study of autobiography that this textbook refuses its limits and attempts to foreground an understanding of America and autobiography as trans-national. Paul John Eakin's claim that 'the true history of American autobiography and the culture in which it is produced and consumed may turn out to be the history of identifiable groups within the culture and of the network of relations among them' is particularly helpful here, although this statement requires significant expansion for the purposes of considering relations *outside* the culture and across national borders (Eakin 1991: 12).

Obama's discussion of the aims of his autobiography is additionally notable for his ambivalence about the act of making the self 's history public – an obvious consequence, if not aim, of autobiography. In a thought-provoking formulation, Alix Kates Shulman describes autobiography as a project in which 'memories are delivered from private custody to the world' (1999: 71). Obama's reluctance suggests that autobiography is a risky enterprise, which threatens an individual's privacy and even consti-tutes some kind of threat. But what kind of threat? It might be that loss of privacy is somehow equated with loss of self. For some of the writers discussed in this volume, autobiography *is* a risky and dangerous act, because of the political statements or claims made (the slave narratives of Frederick Douglass and Harriet Jacobs are dangerous texts in this way). As well as providing another example of the difficulty of separating the self, life and text (publishing autobiography could, conceivably, result in physical harm being done to the autobiographer), this also foregrounds the importance of ethics in autobiography. Writing autobiography neces-sitates ethical decisions and choices (for example, relating to how much information about the self and others one should share). It also often has ethical aims; autobiographers write in order to provide readers with an example of a good life or to improve the lives of others – aims that often intersect with the political aims of many autobiographies.

Katz claims that his task – giving Patty's autobiography to Walter – is to tell 'the dirty truth'. Strikingly, the concept of truth is absent both from Lejeune's definition and from the tripartite structure of the word 'autobiography'. This nicely dramatises a crucial dilemma, with which any scholar of autobiography must grapple: where *is* truth to be found in autobiography? Timothy Dow Adams argues that, in autobiography, '*truth* has been handled in a bewildering variety of ways, including its relation to fiction, nonfiction, fact, fraud, figure, identity, memory, error, and myth' (1990: 1). Is autobiographical truth something that can be proven, quantified? (Legal wrangles provoked by autobiographies might suggest as much.) Is autobiographical truth legal, moral, spiritual or subjective – all of these or more, besides? It *is* all of these, and more besides, on various occasions; it always depends on the particular autobiography being examined (and on who is examining it). Autobiographies are about dependencies and dependents (hence, the importance of relations, and ethics, to autobiography). Each autobiography must be considered on its own terms and in relation to the particular historical and cultural contexts within which it is produced. Readers of autobiography must determine, in Hejinian's phrase, 'what is the meaning hung from that depend' (1987: 28).

Locating truth in autobiography is vital to many readers, because it is the presumed truth of autobiography which makes it not fiction, which makes it identifiable as autobiography. Autobiography is not fiction, because the events in it actually took place – to an individual living in the world, the individual writing the autobiography. Truth is assumed, expected, by the reader, and the autobiographer knows this. It is that presumption of, or commitment to, truth in autobiography which makes autobiography an ethical project. This might seem commonsensical, clear enough, but it is not. The unreliability of memory complicates any individual's claim to tell a truthful story about the past. Obama notes that while his autobiography is indebted to 'contemporaneous journals or the oral histories of my family', 'the dialogue is necessarily an approximation of what was actually said or relayed to me' (2007: xvii). So autobiography has a lot to do with fiction. What of writers like Philip Roth, who invoke questions of autobiographical truth in their fictions by calling fictional characters 'Philip Roth'? For many autobiographers, such as Maxine Hong Kingston, fictions express more profound truths than literal recounting of events. So fiction has a lot to do with autobiography. Indeed, Couser claims that 'the modern novel emerged as an imitation of life writing' (2012: 9–10) – a claim which, while valid, risks diminishing the importance of the fact that life writings are, equally, historical documents. And what about writers like Hejinian or Art Spiegelman, clearly influenced by postmodern and post-structural theory, whose autobiographical texts suggest that truth is provisional, subjective and arrived at via a process of collaboration between writer and reader? Autobiography has a great deal to do with the reader. Indeed, often it is the reader who is the final arbiter of truth, not the autobiographer (the notion of reader as judge of the autobiographer is illustrated by Patty's claim that she is 'worthy of a fresh hearing'). This discussion (which began as a discussion about truth) underscores the point that to study autobiography is to study many different and overlapping sets of relations or dependencies: between autobiographer and reader; between memory, fact and fiction; between truth and reference; between fiction and history.

Autobiography may well be impossible to define; this is because there will, inevitably, be exceptions to any definition. Does this mean that autobiography is impossible? If so, this is not to admit defeat, to be resigned to confusion. It is, in fact, to say a great deal about autobiography. The impasse of explanation that the term 'autobiography' often poses (what is autobiography?) corresponds to the conditions of aporia. Derrida defines aporia as:

> the difficult or the impracticable, here the impossible, passage, the refused, denied, or prohibited passage, indeed the nonpassage, which can in fact be something else, the event of a coming or of a future advent [...] which no longer has the form of the movement that consists in passing, traversing, or transiting. It would be the 'coming to pass' of an event that would no longer have the form or the appearance of a *pas*: in sum, a coming without *pas*. (1993: 8)

Nicholas Royle argues that '"Aporia" is loosely a rhetorical term for "doubt" or "difficulty in choosing" but more precisely it means a sort of absolute blockage, a "No Way", ("aporia" again coming from ancient Greek, a without, poros "way", or "passage")' (2003: 92). As Royle notes, Derrida describes the aporia as an 'interminable experience' and claims that '*the aporia can never simply be endured as such*' (1993: 16, 78). If, as it can sometimes seem in discussions of contemporary autobiography, an autobiographer or critic must choose between, or attempt to reconcile, Enlightenment-influenced or post-structuralist influenced understandings of autobiography (this will be discussed in the third chapter), then this does, indeed, constitute a kind of impasse caused by 'doubt' or 'difficulty in choosing'. To attempt to write an autobiography in the knowledge that certainties about truth and identity do not exist, certainly could be seen as undergoing an 'interminable experience'. However, Derrida's thinking about aporia is useful to consideration of autobiography, in ways that go beyond simply classifying conundrums with which autobiography must engage. When Derrida claims that 'the aporia can never simply be endured as such', he claims the possibility, even necessity, of moving beyond the impasse. It is productive, then, to refuse to attempt to formulate a definition of autobiography, as long as this refusal necessitates considering why refusal is required. This can be addressed, not by thinking about what autobiography is, but by thinking about what autobiography does.

A useful question that can be asked about any autobiography is: 'What is this text's autobiographical occasion?' The phrase 'autobiographical occasion' owes a debt to Sidonie Smith and Julia Watson's 2010 study of autobiography. It refers to the events which may have prompted an autobiographer to undertake the act of producing an autobiography and the rationale he or she presents for doing so. That many autobiographers perceive it necessary to include an explanation of the 'autobiographical occasion' contributes to a situation in which, as Laura Marcus observes, 'attempts to "define" the nature of autobiography are often derived from statements made from within autobiographical texts which are held to have a definitional function, or to operate as statements of intent' (1994: 250). As Anderson notes, Marcus' claim that 'intention' is an important aspect of autobiography is crucial (2011: 2). Often, it is in prefaces, introductions and afterwords that a text's autobiographical occasion is discussed. Marcus notes that Derrida's 'The law of genre' (which will be discussed in the final chapter of this volume) raises 'a problematic recurrent in autobiographical criticism: the relationship between "inside" and "outside"' (1994: 250). Anderson notes this, too, claiming that Derrida questions 'the borders of the text, of what belongs to the "inside" and the "outside"' (2011: 9). The 'autobiographical occasion' is often found at 'the borders of the text' (at the beginning or the end) and shows the permeability of those borders. As Marcus notes, sometimes an autobiography's intention is to close the gap between 'inside' and 'outside' the text (blurring the distinctions between self, life and writing, in ways which are both productive and problematic), but sometimes an autobiography strains to clearly distinguish between 'inside' and outside' (not always successfully, and sometimes the failure is the desired effect). For example, it is vital to note that Patty's autobiographies function as a means of telling the larger story, the novel, in which they exist; to that extent, they are 'outside' the novel's world, apart from it. But her autobiographical narratives have an important part to play *in the text*: they generate some of its most important plot developments (the split with Walter, the reconciliation). Many autobiographies, such as

Benjamin Franklin's, include (additional) examples of autobiographical writing within the autobiography itself (Franklin includes excerpts from his journal), as a means of testifying to the power of autobiography to have real, material effects, as a means of exploring that 'inside/outside' relationship and supporting Margo Culley's claim – made after noting the importance of prefaces and afterwords in autobiography – that 'one feature that distinguishes autobiography from fiction is the persistence, indeed the insistence, with which autobiography talks explicitly about itself' (1992: 18).

Obama's text and Patty's autobiographies reveal the importance of identifying autobiographical occasions. The passage from *Dreams From My Father* quoted above might be understood as one explanation of the text's autobiographical occasion. In addition to fulfilling a desire to communicate renewal of America's democratic promise, though, Obama's text was also occasioned by his achieving the distinction of becoming the first African-American president of the *Harvard Law Review*. As a result, he was approached about writing his autobiography (Obama 2007: vii). However, Obama offers an explanation of this autobiographical occasion (for the first edition of his autobiography, not discussed in detail here) in a preface written on the occasion of the publication of the second edition in 2004. This second edition was occasioned by his securing the Democratic nomination for a seat as the US senator from Illinois (2007: viii). While the first edition of his text is prompted by – and reflects – a focus on Obama's racial identity, the second foregrounds his political ambitions. As Barbara Foley notes, Obama uses the occasion of the second edition to realign its focus in line with those political ambitions; if the first edition stresses Obama's identity as an African-American subject who critiques his culture's constructions of race, the second stresses his identity as transnational, representative American subject and is less critical (Foley 2009: 7–9).

It must be repeated that Patty's autobiographical narratives are fictive. But they, too, have two autobiographical occasions, because they are written years apart. Her first narrative is written as a means of analysing and assuaging the state of mental duress she experiences as a result of her problematic family life. The second is written in an effort to explain herself to Walter and seems a bid to repair their relationship. In one sense, Patty's autobiographical narratives are written primarily for herself. They serve distinctly personal ends. They are thoroughly self-interested (she wants to learn why certain things have happened; she

wants to explain some of her mistakes; she wants Walter to love her). The
first narrative is produced within a therapeutic context. The title explains
that the narrative is written 'at her therapist's suggestion' – a reminder
that personal trauma and distress (such as illness, abuse or bereavement)
constitutes the 'autobiographical occasion' for many autobiographies.
It underscores the therapeutic function many autobiographies have (or
which their writers hope they will have). Patty's use of the third person
in her autobiographical narratives also functions to show estrangement
from self, which might be a marker of her personal distress and her
further objectification within the therapeutic situation.

The use of the third-person autobiographical narrative voice is also,
no doubt, an ironic, parodic acknowledgement of the fact that some
American autobiographies, like that of Henry Adams, are, indeed,
written in the third person. Surely, for Adams and many other autobiographers writing in the twentieth and twenty-first centuries, the use
of irony and parody allows the staging of one strained relationship to
the 'promise' of autobiography (its Enlightenment-influenced models of
identity and truth) and the 'national promise' of democracy. Patty's use
of the third person narrative surely functions, like Adams', to acknowledge how the modern and postmodern subject is a fractured one; operations of capitalism, for example, may well necessitate the objectification
of identity. It also highlights a simple fact often, perhaps, disguised by
use of the first-person voice: in autobiography, a writer treats his or her
(past?) self as an object of study.

The claim that Patty's narrative is written at the behest of the therapist is also parodic. It mocks the dependence on therapy and the confessional, which, for many, is a feature of contemporary American culture
and explains the importance of autobiography within that culture
(Gilmore 2001: 17). It also mocks the tendency of autobiographers to
claim that their narratives are written at the urging or request of others.
Such claims are defensive, and they are present throughout the history
of Western autobiographical writing. Since the subject of an autobiography is (supposedly) the author's self, writers of autobiography have
to acknowledge and defend themselves against readers' suspicions that
they are narcissistic, egotistic and hold excessive belief in their own
importance. Autobiographers have felt the need to anticipate and refute
claims that they write purely for personal gain, whether that takes the
form of fame, public visibility achieved by bringing him or herself to the
attention of others, or financial gain achieved through book sales. Both

Obama and Patty's texts reveal, then, that an autobiography can have multiple, even contradictory, autobiographical occasions, that discussions of autobiographical occasions can be disingenuous (untrustworthy, even) and that they can be revised.

The pressure to refute claims of self-interest as part of discussion of the 'autobiographical occasion' has been, of course, more acute for certain individuals, perhaps especially for female autobiographers. A female autobiographer writing in the eighteenth, nineteenth and early twentieth centuries could expect to encounter readers hostile to her claims to authorship and presumption (or forging) of a place in the public sphere (doing so by writing about her private life, at that).[2] These pressures are by no means absent in the late twentieth and twenty-first centuries, either. For example, Lucy Grealy takes as her autobiographical occasion an illness which leaves her with a disfigurement and a lasting sense that she is 'ugly' – an outsider in a culture in which physical appearance is still a substantial factor. She attempts to refuse a valuation of women as objects of the male gaze, not self-fashioning subjects.

The need of autobiographers to explain that they write not only for self-interest suggests that to produce autobiography is to engage in an enterprise of dubious ethical merit. This relates to the question of whose interests are being served by a particular autobiography. 'Interests' of all sorts are important to autobiography, too, and this is especially apparent when considering the concept of 'representativeness' in autobiography, which will be discussed in the second chapter. It is often difficult, for example, not to think that Patty is writing mainly in an effort to deny responsibility for her mistakes, a sense only (ironically) exacerbated, in fact, by the fact that her autobiography is, in many ways, an exercise in self-blame. Another important claim made in this study is that the ethical intent of American autobiographies is of vital significance. The intensely ethical and political aims of many of these autobiographies might be understood as a commitment on the part of many autobiographers to explore how their autobiographies can do good, particularly in relation to how a particular text explores its subject's relationship to the 'national promise'. This *might* be what marks them out as distinctively American. This is a possibly tautological claim, which is made with great caution.

There are two primary strategies by which this ethical and political intent is made manifest in many American autobiographies. They are of equal importance, and that they are both highly ambivalent is significant. That Katz's gesture of giving Patty's autobiography to Walter is both a good deed and a bad one is illustrative of this ambivalence. Firstly, American autobiographers frequently make a gesture of offering themselves, or, more specifically, their autobiographies, to their readers. That is, it is claimed that writing about oneself will further the interests of others. The story of an autobiographer's life is presented as a model for readers; for the purposes of emulation, perhaps, or (also) in a cautionary spirit, so that readers can avoid errors the autobiographer made. Benjamin Franklin's autobiography is one of the best-known examples of a text which offers the self as model (in its claims that 'mistakes were made', Patty's narrative is surely also ironically acknowledging Franklin's famous use of the trope of 'errata'). However, whether Franklin's gesture is altruistic is debatable. To offer oneself as a model for others is a highly self-regarding gesture. Secondly, some of the most well-known American autobiographers have written in order to give voice to particular identity groups which the writer believes to be oppressed or insufficiently visible. This, too, could be understood as self-regarding, because often the autobiographer identifies with, or belongs to, the group he or she is trying to bring to prominence. Both of these ethical strategies are pressed into the service of fulfilling the political intent of American autobiographies: staging a relation to the American 'national promise'. This political intent is also an ethical one, of course.

The two ethical aims listed above suggest that autobiography can be understood as taking on many of the qualities of a gift (Katz leaves Patty's autobiography on Walter's bed as a 'parting gift'). For Derrida, the gift is an aporia, because it partakes of the impossible: 'For there to be a gift, there must be no reciprocity, return, exchange, countergift, or debt'. This is because '[i]f the other gives me back or owes me or has to give me back what I give him or her, there will not have been a gift, whether this restitution is immediate or whether it is programmed by a complex calculation of a long-term deferral or difference' (Derrida 1992: 12). Gift-giving, then, is ethically ambivalent. Significantly, it is through a gesture of refusal – refusal to participate in this economy, a placing of oneself 'outside' it – which presents a means of escaping from the 'interminable experience' of the aporia. Refusal is expressed via the gesture of return, which Derrida prohibits: '[The gift] must not circulate, it must not be exchanged, it must not in any case be exhausted, as a gift, by the process of exchange, by the movement of the circle in the form of return to the point of departure' (1992: 12). Derrida argues that:

> The simple intention to give, insofar as it carries the intentional meaning
> of the gift, suffices to make a return payment to oneself. The simple
> consciousness of the gift right away sends itself back the gratifying
> image of goodness or generosity, of the giving-being who, knowing
> itself to be such, recognises itself in a circular, specular fashion, in a sort
> of auto-recognition, self-approval, and narcissistic gratitude. (1992: 23)

Derrida does, however, specify conditions under which it possible to
give a gift: 'For there to be a gift, *it is necessary* [*il faut*] that the donee
not give back, amortize, reimburse, acquit himself, enter into a contract,
and that he never have contracted a debt' (1992: 13). What Derrida
calls the 'impossibility or double bind of the gift' is expressed in the
claim that: 'For there to be a gift, it is necessary that the gift not even
appear, that it not be perceived or received as gift' (1992: 16). A form of
non-passive endurance of the aporias of autobiography arises from the
conceptualisation of autobiography itself as a gift – a gift which is always
attempting to refuse the appellation of itself as 'gift'. Consideration of
autobiography as gift emphasises the complex interpersonal relationships involved in the autobiographical project and the fact that they are
usually ethically compromised.

   The fact that no textbook on American autobiography exists (until
now) signifies another impasse: a critical one, this time. If 'autobiography' is difficult to define, then 'American autobiography' is even more
so. The absence of a textbook on American autobiography probably
signifies critical reluctance to engage in discussions of the 'Americanness' of autobiography; there are fears that this focus involves reductive, essentialist notions of the subject who writes. Although leading
scholars in the study of autobiography, such as Paul John Eakin, G.
Thomas Couser, Leigh Gilmore and Nancy Miller, primarily consider
American texts (indeed, American texts probably comprise a majority
of titles considered in scholarly studies of autobiography), no recent
textbooks take American autobiographies as their subject. It seems that,
at present, American autobiographies are more likely to be considered
under other frameworks: as works by women, by African-Americans,
or by postmodern or postcolonial writers, for example. For a focus on
American autobiography, students must look to a group of critical works
published in the 1980s and 1990s, to texts such as Couser's *Altered Egos:
Authority in American Autobiography* (1989), Timothy Dow Adams'
Telling Lies in Modern American Autobiography (1990), or to collections

of essays edited by Arthur E. Stone – *The American Autobiography: A Collection of Critical Essays* (1981) – and Eakin – *American Autobiography: Retrospect and Prospect* (1991). These critical works are no longer innovative. And while they do make provocative (and problematic) claims about the possibility of understanding autobiography as a particularly 'American' genre, none is designed to offer students a guide to the topic.

Those claims made in many of the texts above – that autobiography is somehow a particularly 'American' genre – constitute one significant cause of the critical impasse which study of American autobiography appears to have reached. To support those claims, those works focus overwhelmingly on the same few autobiographies, particularly those written by Benjamin Franklin, Henry David Thoreau, Frederick Douglass and Henry Adams. They focus overwhelmingly on the male subject and the American tradition of the 'self-made man' exemplified by these autobiographies. And, in a tautological move, they claim that these texts reveal autobiography to be particularly 'American', because they reflect these American ideologies. While these texts and ideologies are unquestionably important within the history of autobiographical writing in America and will be discussed in this textbook, the problematic nature of what has often constituted the 'canon' of American autobiography must be acknowledged and ways of moving beyond the critical impasse must be suggested.

Couser's *Altered Egos* provides a good example of this impasse. Couser attempts to engage with post-structuralist notions of the death of the author and their consequences for understanding the self and writing, but he is reluctant to surrender essentialist notions of what is meant by 'American' (to claim autobiography is particularly 'American' is often to invoke essentialist notions of American identity). This reluctance results in a text poised uneasily between a post-structuralist understanding of autobiography and an understanding of autobiography which remains influenced by notions of coherent identity and accessible truth, as informed by Enlightenment philosophy (a tension, incidentally, with which any contemporary critic of autobiography must engage). Fascinatingly, Couser's most recent work privileges the term 'memoir' and yet, nonetheless, contains chapters focusing particularly on texts (such as Franklin's, Stein's and the slave narrative) which have been understood as canonical American autobiographies. This focus is designed to support the book's assumption, expressed in one chapter title, of 'Memoir's American Roots', perhaps suggesting that these tensions remain (Couser: 2012). This tension must be confronted in a textbook on American autobiography, not only in order to consider the difficulties of reading and writing the autobiographical American 'I', but in order to think about the 'Americanness' of autobiography.

This textbook aims to provide students with a comprehensive and informative guide to the history and importance of autobiographical writing in America. Many of the texts discussed in this textbook are 'limit-cases' (Gilmore 2001: 7), in that they might not be easily incorporated by, or actively resist, Lejeune's definitions, together with the label 'autobiography' – and even that of 'America', for that matter. All the texts discussed in the first chapter of this textbook (Rowlandson, Franklin, Equiano, Douglass, Jacobs) were written before the term 'autobiography' was widely used. Anderson notes that one of the earliest uses of the term is by the English poet Robert Southey in 1809 (2011: 6). The history of autobiography in the West, as noted, is a product of Enlightenment ideologies and to write autobiography may necessarily involve engaging with these, especially as they pertain to the concepts of identity and truth. If autobiography in Western culture has origins in European philosophies, then, surely, any claims that autobiography is especially 'American' need to be treated with scepticism.

Lejeune's definition of autobiography has value, in that its description of a specifically masculine subject and a specific model of identity may accurately reflect the only kind of subject (male) who has consistently been granted the ability to write autobiography and, perhaps, the only kind of subject for whom the label 'autobiography' is appropriate. The history of autobiography production in Western cultures is a history of exclusions and inclusions. In its valorisation of the white male subject and his history, autobiography has often excluded members of various identity groups (such as women, African-Americans) from consideration and value. But, paradoxically, the history of autobiography is also marked by the efforts of practitioners who belong to those excluded groups and who use autobiography to make various claims. They make claims about their status as 'real persons'; about their abilities to tell the truth and their desire to tell certain truths; about their abilities to speak on behalf of others, to represent various others. The history of autobiography can, therefore, be understood as marked by a series of interventions on the part of individuals who seek to stretch the limits of how autobiography is conventionally understood or even, perhaps, to take leave of the term altogether.

The history of autobiography can also be understood as marked by
a series of complex gestures of refusal. Autobiographers have written to
passionately affirm the value of their own identities and voices; often,
this has entailed passionate refutation of the identities and values granted
to them by others. Autobiographies may well be, as Gilmore notes,
crucially about self-representation, but the critical history of autobiography largely concerns the definitions and classifications imposed on
certain texts by their readers, whose decisions will, of course, be determined by the ways in which autobiographers' acts of self-representation
are read (and readers often refuse to agree on how they are read). Strikingly, very few autobiographies discussed in this volume explicitly claim
to be 'autobiography'. Gertrude Stein's *The Autobiography of Alice B.
Toklas* (1933) openly declares itself to be autobiography, but only in its
final paragraph and under conditions which may render its own claim
redundant. Lyn Hejinian's prose-poem, *My Life*, refers to 'the lobes of
autobiography' (1987: 28), but the reference is passive, circumspect:
the speaker does not say 'the lobes of *my* autobiography'. In Franzen's
Freedom, Patty is untroubled by the label 'autobiography', but as she is
fictional, her texts are thoroughly problematic.

   This volume consists of four chapters, each framed around a central
thematic: the first two focus on 'Properties', the third on 'Gifts and
Giving' and the fourth on 'Recoveries'. These thematics facilitate
engagement with questions ('properties') central to autobiography
– those of definition, identity, relationships, representation, agency,
intention, the law, ethics of writing autobiography, truth, reference,
and genre. The first two chapters focus on 'Exemplary Subjects'. They
introduce students to important early autobiographical narratives, to the
major modes of American autobiographical writing in the eighteenth,
nineteenth and early twentieth centuries, and to a selection of notable
practitioners of the genre. The first chapter introduces students to
the transnational colonial subject (Olaudah Equiano), the Puritan
captivity narrative (Mary Rowlandson), the narrative of the 'self-made
man'(Benjamin Franklin) and the nineteenth century slave narrative
(Frederick Douglass and Harriet Jacobs). The second chapter considers
the confusing conundrum of 'representativeness' in autobiography, by
examining works by Henry David Thoreau, Walt Whitman, Henry
Adams and Gertrude Stein. While aiming to provide students with a
survey of American autobiographical writing, it will be made clear that
the processes by which these texts and their authors have been rendered

representatively 'American' are problematic; in the first chapter, this is primarily because many of the autobiographies cannot be understood as American, and in the second chapter, this is primarily because of what is at stake in the issue of representation.

The third and fourth chapters, focusing on 'Contemporary Subjects', consider autobiographies published after 1970 – a date chosen because it was from around this period that post-structuralism affected understandings of the subject who could write and conceptions of truth, identity and reference in autobiography (Anderson 2011: 5–6; Smith 1987). The third chapter aims to introduce students to the central factors influencing American autobiography and autobiography criticism since the 1970s, which arguably stem from developments in post-structuralist theory. The texts discussed here – Maxine Hong Kingston's *A Woman Warrior* (1977) and Art Spiegelman's *Maus* (1996) – register the fact that contemporary American autobiography often highlights the plight of, or simply explores, the voices and experiences of so-called 'minority' or marginalised identity groups. Kingston's and Spiegelman's texts consider the complicated ethical relationships of self to other (hence, the emphasis on 'gifts and giving') and share concerns with hybrid or mixed genres, particularly via the inclusion of the photograph. This chapter acknowledges that an understanding of identity as relational, a concern with ethics in life writing and the relation of photography to autobiography currently receive particular critical attention. The fourth chapter considers the current importance of illness and/or disability in life writing, in the context of the 'memoir boom' in Western cultures in the 1990s and beyond. It examines Lucy Grealy's *Autobiography of a Face* (1994) and Lance Armstrong's *It's Not About the Bike* (2001) to consider the relationship of gender to genre and the importance of the gesture of refusal in autobiography.

As this description indicates, this discussion of autobiography takes a broadly chronological shape. However, this volume refuses to offer a history of autobiography which is linear, definitive or exhaustive. Sedgwick's meditation on the preposition 'beside' can help to clarify the designs (in all senses) of this textbook:

> *Beside* is an interesting preposition also because there's nothing very dualistic about it; a number of elements may lie alongside one another, though not an infinity of them. *Beside* permits a spacious agnosticism about several of the linear logics that enforce dualistic thinking: noncontradication or the law of the excluded middle, cause versus

affect, subject versus object. Its interest does not, however, depend on a fantasy of metonymically egalitarian or even pacific relations, as any child knows who's shared a bed with siblings. *Beside* comprises a wide range of desiring, identifying, representing, repelling, paralleling, differentiating, rivaling, leaning, twisting, mimicking, withdrawing, attracting, aggressing, warping, and other relations. (2003: 8)

The chapters of this text, and the autobiographies discussed within those chapters, should be understood to 'lie alongside' each other in exactly the way Sedgwick describes – existing in the same multiple, uncomfortable relations. These relations are embedded within the word 'autobiography' itself; its three parts (self, life, writing) lie awkwardly alongside each other. To examine just how they 'lie alongside' each other is the study of autobiography. This textbook conducts this study in ways which necessitate engagement with the 'wide range' of 'other relations' Sedgwick describes, which, hopefully, move beyond the dualistic thinking often cited as restricting the study of autobiography (truth/ lies, fiction/history, inside/outside).

This textbook cannot discuss every important American autobiography, so the stories it tells and the relations it describes are also, necessarily, marked by exclusions. The texts included within its pages are not representative of the 'best' or most important American autobiographies; they are chosen because they introduce students to (some) major practitioners and properties (thematic concepts and interpretative difficulties) necessary to the study of autobiography. It is worth, too, pointing out some of my own 'interests' – in youth and ageing, in American culture from the 1950s to the present – because these, unavoidably, influence the decisions to focus on certain texts and the nature of the readings offered (as Gilmore notes, the autobiographical 'I' makes its appearance in many contexts, not just in autobiographies). My interests in autobiographies by women and in feminist criticism explain the presence of Denise Riley's *The Words of Selves* and Sedgwick's *Touching Feeling*, in particular, throughout this textbook. These critics have guided much of my thought on autobiography, even if they were not explicitly discussing that topic.

Finally, to Sedgwick's itemisation of the different kinds of relations which the word 'beside' invokes, the word 'tilting' must be added. Laura Doyle suggests that transnational studies, understood as the 'transports and transformations that occur across the borders of nations', might track the *'regional tilt* of these flows and dynamics, of nations-in-relation'

(2009: 4). Doyle's focus on the 'regional' does not concern me here, but her use of the word 'tilt' does. 'Tilt' is described in the Oxford English Dictionary as: 'to cause to fall; to thrust, push, throw down or over; to overthrow, overturn, upset' and also as: 'to cause to lean abruptly from the vertical or incline abruptly from the horizontal; to slope, slant'. These relations describe the ways in which the autobiographies described in these pages move towards and away from each other, pulled by attractions, repulsions and absences, and the ways in which they orient themselves, in relation to autobiography's Enlightenment influences. 'Tilt' also describes the ways in which consideration of 'America' and 'autobiography' involves an orientation (slant) towards 'other' things (other nations, other genres or disciplines). For example, this textbook on American autobiography begins with discussion of a fiction and ends with discussion of a scene in Europe. Finally, 'tilt' describes the ways in which this textbook offers unsettled and unsettling readings of autobiography and America as plural, provisional, partial and more besides.

Notes

1. For recent, much more inclusive studies of memoir, which note, and may also perpetuate, that conflation (or confusion) of the terms 'memoir' and 'autobiography', see Yagoda (2010); Couser (2012).
2. For important, useful, general studies of women's autobiography, see Smith (1987); Culley (1992); Swindells (1995); Smith and Watson (1998); Smith and Watson (2010). For studies of women's autobiographical writing in the eighteenth and nineteenth centuries, see Nussbaum (1989) and Fabian (2000).

PART ONE

Exemplary Subjects

CHAPTER I

Spiritual, Secular and Enslaved Selves

Autobiography could easily be called the essential American genre, a form of writing closely allied to our national self-consciousness. (Parini 1999: 11)

Naturally a great deal of self-presentation is asking, if somewhat hopelessly, 'Love me'. But first the identifications which go into my self-portrayal have exerted a kind of productive alienation, for I find my affinity with something outside me only by moving towards and accepting some externally given account of a self, which I then take home as mine. This can be a happy acquisition: Later I may burnish myself up a bit, until I can see the gleam of my own reflection in myself. (Riley 2000: 2)

With the claim above, Jay Parini begins his editor's preface to *The Norton Anthology of American Autobiography*. This textbook begins by refusing Parini's claim. Autobiography *cannot* be called 'the essential American genre'; not easily and not in the reductive ways Parini suggests.

Parini argues that autobiography is a genre which has particular affinities with American cultural identity. Denise Riley begins her critical study, *The Words of Selves*, by considering what is at stake in any complicated linguistic act of self-presentation. Her discussion is pertinent to autobiography, which can be understood, of course, as an exercise in self-presentation. Lest Riley's speculations do not seem immediately relevant to Parini's argument, consider his use of the word 'our', suggesting that self-description is, indeed, operative here. Parini's claim that autobiography is the 'essential American genre' is dependent upon acceptance of an 'externally given account of a self'; in this case, an essentialist, mythologised and exceptionalist version of American national identity which Parini has 'taken home', in the sense that he accepts, identifies with and locates himself within that version. His claim that autobiography is particularly 'American' celebrates that version of American identity (his self-presentation effectively says 'love America'). And this celebrated version of American identity is, in turn, used to explain why American autobiographies (in particular, the texts chosen as worthy of inclusion in his anthology) are valuable and important (his self-presentation also says, 'love American autobiographies'). Citing autobiographies by Benjamin Franklin, Henry David Thoreau, Mark Twain, Henry Douglass and Henry Adams as integral to 'any shortlist of classic American texts', Parini adds that these texts 'would muscle aside most American novels or volumes of poetry of the same period' (1999: 11). The language of masculinist competitiveness here is telling; for Parini, asserting the value of American autobiographies in general (and some, in particular) apparently involves exclusion and devaluing – muscling aside – other identities and genres (American poetry and novels, women writers, non-American texts?).

Parini's claims about the close relationship between America and autobiography are well-established. Many critics have argued that autobiography, concerned with questions of identity, has a special place within a culture which prizes individualism and which is preoccupied with identity formation. For example, Robert F. Sayre argues that autobiographies offer 'a broader and more direct contact with American experience than any other kind of writing', because they have been written 'in almost every part of the country', by a great many different people (Sayre, in Stone 1981: 11). Sayre offers a partial list of the kinds of individuals who have written autobiography:

> presidents and thieves, judges and professors, Indians and immigrants (of nearly every nationality), by ex-slaves and slaveowners, by men and women in practically every line of work, abolitionists to zoo-keepers, by adolescents and octogenarians, counterfeiters, captives, muggers, muckrakers, preachers, and everybody else. (Sayre, in Stone 1981: 11)

He adds that: 'The catalogue is as great as one of Walt Whitman's own ... or greater. It is the true Song of Myself. And Ourselves' (Sayre, in Stone 1981: 11). Parini develops his argument for autobiography as 'the essential American genre', as follows:

> It should perhaps have come as no surprise that autobiography would become a central, even dominant, form of writing in a society devoted, at least in principle, to the notion of radical equality: democracy presupposes a social context in which the individual is not only valued but pre-eminent and also representative. That is, the individual

member (in literature as in politics) *stands in* for the group, suggesting
that his or her experience is general. (1999: 11)

Parini's 'at least in principle' suggests that commitment to 'radical
equality' is problematic. Parini avoids extensive consideration of the
'alienation' described by Riley – alienation caused by the awareness that
to take on any identification (here, to identify as 'American', in Parini's
terms) is to acknowledge that what is being 'taken home', or identified
with, is external to the self, other. To push this logic to an extreme, it
is false. Awareness of this alienation is 'productive', in Riley's terms,
because it involves acknowledging that what it means to be 'American'
is far from simple; it necessitates admitting that the version of American
identity Parini invokes is only one of many and his gesture of self-
description contradictory (to assume an externally given identity surely
undercuts the uniqueness and individuality perceived to be an integral
feature of American identity). It would require interrogating the ideologies which contribute to the special status of the American identity he
invokes.

The 'productive alienation' described above is important to the acts
of self-description undertaken by every autobiography discussed in this
chapter: Mary Rowlandson's *Narrative of the Captivity and Restoration of
Mrs. Mary Rowlandson* (1682), Benjamin Franklin's *The Autobiography*
(1771–1790), Olaudah Equiano's *The Interesting Narrative of the Life
of Olaudah Equiano, or Gustavus Vassa, the African* (1789), Frederick
Douglass' *Narrative of the Life of Frederick Douglass, an American Slave*
(1845) and Harriet Jacobs' *Incidents in the Life of a Slave Girl* (1861). Self-
description is not a 'happy acquisition' (in the sense of being joyful or
simple) for any of these writers, with the possible exception of Franklin.
Significantly, it is Franklin who is the most comfortably understood
within the version of 'American' that Parini celebrates. Parini says that:

American literature begins with Benjamin Franklin. Before that, there
was colonial literature. And though we have earlier memoirs [...] the
genre of autobiography does not properly begin until Franklin writes
the history of a self-created life [...]. (1999: 13)

Understanding American autobiography as beginning with Franklin
only has validity in respect to the narrowly construed version of
American identity Parini decides to 'take home'; it also involves more
than a little creative selectivity when it comes to labelling texts 'autobiography'. Franklin did not label his own work as autobiography. The word

'autobiography' did not come into wide circulation until the nineteenth century, possibly coined by Robert Southey in 1809 (Anderson 2011: 6). It is, therefore, ironic that the text rendered the paramount exemplar of American autobiography should be given the label of 'autobiography' externally, by others. If Franklin's work can be labelled autobiography retrospectively, then why not the 'colonial literature' which precedes his, such as Mary Rowlandson's?

If it is difficult to locate the place where autobiography begins, it is also, for the purposes of this project, difficult to define where or when 'American' might begin. For example, the autobiographies of Rowlandson and Equiano interrogate the devotion to 'radical equality' promised by the democratic societies in which each spends some part of their lives – a preoccupation Parini claims to be particularly 'American'. In both texts, the individual (Rowlandson and Equiano, as autobiographers) 'is not only valued but pre-eminent and also representative' (Parini 1999: 11). It is problematic to understand autobiography as a particularly 'American' genre, because the earliest examples of autobiographical writing in Western culture (that is, not only in America) are influenced by (made possible by, even) Enlightenment (European) philosophical thought about identity and truth. The development of the modern sovereign subject and of autobiography occurs in the same period; early examples of autobiography record and legitimate the construction of that subject.

This textbook suggests that instead of the uncritical acceptance of ideologies of individualism and American exceptionalism, which seem to define 'American autobiography' for Parini, it is the *questioning* of democratic principles and the (often related) refusal to accept definitions of identity attributed by others that might mark something called 'American autobiography' and give it its political and ethical impetus. Additionally, awareness of autobiography's European influences suggests that American autobiography must be understood within the context of the transnational, in Laura Doyle's terms:

> In the kind of transnational studies I highlight here, the focus is less strictly on the movements of people and capital across national borders and more on the implicitly other-oriented interactions between and among nations, making them mutually shaping and mutually contingent phenomena. In this model, there certainly are nations – they are still with us clearly – but there is no *a priori*, Herderian spirit, or purely indigenous liberatory 'inside' of the nation: rather there

are radically co-formed nations, arising from material and ideological forces that continuously transform the existence of both or all national sides. (2009: 1)

American autobiographies are transnational autobiographies. The dependence of American autobiography upon European, Enlightenment-influenced models of sovereign identity and narrative (such as the *bildungsroman*, for example) constitutes only one of many ways in which American autobiographies reveal 'other-oriented interactions' and are concerned with *relations* of many kinds. Doyle prioritises the importance of multiple kinds of relations in her understanding of the transnational as 'dialectical philosophy':

> I should note, too, that in my approach a dialectical philosophy is not inherently a philosophy of the double or the dyad. Although the prefix *dia* has associations with two because of its roots in the Greek word for that number, in Greek *dia* also has the ancient meanings of *across*, *through*, and *thoroughly*. It works as a preposition or prefix indicating relation across difference or separateness. (2009: 2)

Reading the autobiographies chosen for discussion in this textbook as transnational avoids a dangerous re-inscription of the exceptionalist ideology, which has made many critical studies of American autobiography reductive and exclusive. Critical discussions of American autobiography have tended to itemise the same list of notable figures, making Parini's circular argument: Franklin's (or Douglass' or Thoreau's or Adams') autobiography is an important American autobiography, because it describes certain ideologies and values, which have been constructed as American and important. The autobiographies studied in this chapter are transnational, in that they describe subjects whose lives and identities are constructed within various processes of colonial enterprise (Doyle's 'movements of people and capital across national borders'). They also share an exploration of the conception of identity as property, something alluded to by Riley's reference to self-description as a (potentially) 'happy acquisition'. Lauren Berlant outlines how American identity has been constructed as, and around, the concept of property:

> Here is a brief story about the history of birthright citizenship in the United States, beginning with a familiar kind of long view. In the eighteenth century, the United States came into being via a democratic

revolution against a geographically distant monarchial authority and
an economically aggressive colonial marginality. The fantasy of a
national democracy was based on principles of abstract personhood
(all persons shall be formally equivalent) and its rational representation in a centralised state and federal system. The constitutional
American 'person' was a white male property owner: more than that,
though, was unenumerated in the law.

These abstract principles of democratic nationality have always
been hypocritical. From the beginning, entre populations of persons
were excluded from the national promise which, because it was a
promise, was held out paradoxically: falsely, as a democratic reality,
and legitimately, as a promise, the promise that the democratic
citizenship form makes to people caught in history. The populations
who were and are managed by the discipline of the promise – women,
African Americans, Native Americans, immigrants, homosexuals –
have long experienced simultaneously the wish to be full citizens and
the violence of their partial citizenship. Of course, the rules of citizenship constantly change, both in the law and in the public sense of
how persons ought to be treated, protected, and encouraged to act.
But it is not false to say that over the long term some of us have been
American enough to provide labor but not American enough to be
sustained by the fullest resources of democratic national privilege.
(1997: 18–19)

In very different ways, informed by vastly disparate historical and
cultural contexts, each writer discussed in this chapter conceives of,
or counters conceptions of, him or herself as property, in ways which
conform to, and collide with, the 'abstract principles of democratic
nationality' that Berlant outlines. For example, in describing himself as
a sovereign self, Franklin claims the act of self-description (his identity
is his property), while all of the other writers discussed in this chapter
contest constructions of themselves as the property of others. This
determines the political and ethical claims of these texts: for example,
Douglass and Jacobs challenge those principles of democratic nationality, by claiming social equality and a human identity within a culture
which does not grant them personhood or subject status at all. By so
doing, they protest and contest dominant constructions of identity in the
societies in which they live. The aim of this chapter is, then, to introduce
students to a selection (and it must be stressed that it is only a selection)
of notable early autobiographies and to consider, more generally, some

of the 'properties' of (American?) autobiography, many of which will receive further discussion in subsequent chapters.

Mary Rowlandson's *Narrative of the Captivity and Restoration of Mrs. Mary Rowlandson* (1682) is one of the most important captivity narratives of the seventeenth century. Rowlandson recounts the experience of being taken captive by Native Americans, during a raid on the colonial settlement of Lancaster, New England, in 1676. Andrea Tinnemeyer argues that:

> captivity was, in the Puritan mindset, a testing of the victim's moral rectitude and worthiness as elect; accordingly, reading a captivity made the reader a surrogate to the same trials and tribulations and reinforced religious conviction for those among the flock who were straying or backsliding. (2006: xii)

Rowlandson's text constitutes an ambiguous meditation on the lessons drawn from her experience, the properties of identity and the self as property; her capture transforms her from a highly regarded member of her Puritan community to the property of her captors – a valuable commodity. The experience of captivity constitutes one primary aspect of what could be called the 'autobiographical occasion' of her text. The term 'autobiographical occasion' owes much to the work of Sidonie Smith and Julia Watson, who note that 'sites of storytelling' can be considered as 'occasional and locational' (2010: 69). A text's 'sites of storytelling' comprise its autobiographical occasion(s), and these can be identified by asking the following questions: What has motivated the autobiographer to write his or her text at this time? As Smith and Watson's comments suggest, any autobiography is likely to have more than one 'autobiographical occasion'.

Rowlandson's autobiography purports to describe her literal and spiritual 'restoration', with the intent of providing edification and spiritual consolation for her religious community, of whom she is cast as representative. She therefore provides an early example of an 'exemplary self', which Ruth A. Banes describes as 'the prevailing autobiographical persona during the eighteenth and nineteenth centuries' (1982: 226–7). Banes describes how autobiographers conform to this exemplary pattern; they:

> fit their individual histories into a preconceived pattern: religious, political, or mythical. The conventional pattern includes three devices: apologetic openings, parable form, and the purposes of Divine

Providence. These work together to explain and justify writing about oneself. By continuing a tradition which seventeenth-century spiritual autobiographers had established, eighteenth-century autobiographers were able to justify the act of writing of oneself to an audience which was not yet familiar with the distinct and identifiable form, known today as autobiography. (1982: 227)

While Banes discusses the eighteenth century, in particular, those anxieties about justifying the act of writing about one's self, together with the apologetic or defensive explanations such anxieties generate, constitute important properties of autobiography. These are evidenced throughout the history of autobiographical writing and probably explain why many autobiographies draw attention to their autobiographical occasion(s). That these properties are complex and problematic and occur in many guises will be illustrated in subsequent chapters. They are present, too, in Rowlandson's text, finding their locus in that term 'restoration'. As Lisa Logan notes, 'the work of Rowlandson's text is to reestablish a social, ideological and discursive "home" for her', with the purpose of 'restoring Rowlandson's position among her "Christian friends"' (1993: 258). In Riley's terms, the objective of Rowlandson's autobiography is to engage in an act of self-description, which enables Rowlandson to be successfully assimilated within her community in the aftermath of her captivity. Rowlandson ostensibly wishes to 'take home', to claim as her own, a description of herself as 'Puritan'. But is Rowlandson 'restored'? If so, at what cost?

The price of Rowlandson's 'restoration' may be that her experiences, and even her text, may not be her own. This is clear from the beginning:

The sovereignty and goodness of GOD, together with the faithfulness of his promises displayed, being a narrative of the captivity and restoration of Mrs. Mary Rowlandson, commended by her, to all that desires to know the Lord's doings to, and dealings with her. Especially to her dear children and relations. The second Addition Corrected and Amended. Written by her own hand for her private use, and now made public at the earnest desire of some friends, and for the benefit of the afflicted. Deut. 32.39. See now that I, even I am he, and there is no god with me, I kill and I make alive, I wound and I heal, neither is there any can deliver out of my hand. ([1682] 2007: 7)

Rowlandson's title contains several features common to seventeenth- and eighteenth-century spiritual autobiographies. It declares the text an

illustration of God's favour – the workings of Providence. It prioritises
the pursuit of spiritual truths. It is designed for edification of others. It
is written retrospectively. It treats the writer's life in generalised terms
(Shea 1968: ix–x). Yet, this text (and the title above) is riven by tensions,
some endemic to spiritual autobiography and some specific to Rowlandson's text. In offering herself (or being offered) to her community as
its exemplar, Rowlandson's experiences illustrate the Puritan use of
typology – an interpretive practice described by Deborah Madsen 'as a
prime means by which [the Puritan colonists] could measure the success
of their mission in the New World' (1998: 6). Rowlandson's narrative is
to be understood as allegorical, representative of the trials and tribula-
tions of life in the New World, providing evidence of God's promise
to care for the colonists (2007: 4–6). Banes claims that some eighteenth-century autobiographies 'synthesise private and public histories
in accordance with the dominant ideals of eighteenth century America'
(1982: 227), but Rowlandson's seventeenth-century autobiography
achieves a similar synthesis through its use of typology. Or perhaps it
only strives to achieve that synthesis? Or perhaps it does not strive for
synthesis? The qualities allowing Rowlandson to be exemplary – her
innocence, her role as beleaguered and passive sufferer and victim –
pertain to her gender. And these properties describe the struggles of
her New World Puritan community. But by publically calling attention to her individual experiences, Rowlandson threatens to undermine
the construction of herself as exemplary – a sufferer who desires only
self-effacement, union of self with God. Self-effacement should mark
Rowlandson as a dutiful female member of her community, and it is
suggested, as s[he] claims, that her narrative is offered to (the property
of) God and that she makes her narrative public at the desire of others;
she does not write for self-interest. However, as a female writer claiming
a public voice and role, Rowlandson flouts her community's standards of
appropriate behaviour for women. Finally, while her experience appears
to reaffirm her faith and values, the text hints that Rowlandson is not
wholly accepting of the values of her community or her place within
it. The fact that Rowlandson is viewed as property in both communities – her value and status within her Puritan community, upon which
her captors trade, is determined by that of her husband's status (he is a
minister), and she is bought back from her captors for the sum of 'twenty
pounds, the price of my redemption' ([1682] 2007: 48) – a underscores
affinities, rather than differences, between the values of Rowlandson's

community and those of her captors and troubles the purported aims of her narrative (to demonstrate the superiority and distinctive nature of her own community).

Daniel B. Shea poses a problem for spiritual autobiography: 'Could the self ever be banished from first-person narrative?' (1968: 14). If the self cannot be banished from an autobiography in which the aim is precisely to lose one's identity in union with God, then spiritual autobiographies are records of the sinful state of the autobiographer. Later in his study, Shea asks the same question differently: 'How far does autobiography of any sort allow itself to be put to specialised uses while remaining autobiography? Most American autobiography [...] has aimed at some form of edification. At least, it has framed an argument, a recommendation, a special plea of some sort' (1968: 94). First-person narrative binds the autobiographer to the self, which it is the autobiographer's spiritual duty to transcend. The inevitable failure this implies might be illustrated by the fact that despite Rowlandson's text's claim to be primarily a demonstration of, and expression of thanks for, God's protection, the narrative also has thoroughly self-interested, earthly designs; Rowlandson's 'restoration' refers to her successful return to her community. That Rowlandson could still be 'at home' within her Puritan community is something her readers, members of that community, may have needed convincing of. Her period of captivity, spent among a group described as 'barbarous creatures', whose activities create a 'lively resemblance of hell' ([1982] 2007: 10), would surely function to estrange her. To the extent that Rowlandson wishes to argue for her restoration within her community, the aim of Rowlandson's narrative is to underline continuity, to testify that she remains the same person. Her desire for earthly restoration compromises her simultaneous wish to claim spiritual restoration – to argue that her experiences have changed her for good. Here, Rowlandson's text illustrates a paradoxical property of autobiography: while many autobiographers write to claim exceptional status, because of the transformations in identity they have undergone, many autobiographies are equally likely to locate that exceptional status in a claim to be unchanged by experience. These oppositional tendencies speak to profound questions about the nature of identity (identity as innate? Essential? Provisional? Constructed?), with which autobiographies inevitably engage. In Rowlandson's text, as in many autobiographies, both desires (for the self to be recognised as both unchanged and transformed) exist simultaneously and in tension.

The biblical allusion which concludes the title, above, further suggests that this is a text straining to contain and reconcile the tensions expressed by its subject. The text's numerous scriptural references ostensibly explicate Rowlandson's experience, by constructing biblical allegories for it (an example of the use of typology). They support, by furnishing evidence for, the contention that she has received God's favour and protection, and they establish her as a devout, informed Puritan – one skilled in reading her world and her experiences, who deserves to be read as exemplary. Logan argues that the biblical verses function as:

> 'places' that comfort and provide reassurance in an uncertain world; they serve as secure textual positions, discursive anchors that help [Rowlandson] to make sense of her sorrow by placing her experience in the wilderness into a typological and, therefore, meaningful (for her) context. (1993: 255)

There is much substance to this argument, but the scriptural refer-ences are ambiguous and can usually be read as both supporting and undermining the Puritan faith; they are less secure 'places' than Logan suggests. Michelle Burnham usefully refers to 'the curious split' in narrative voice and tone created by the biblical references and suggests different ways of conceptualising the divide they create between physical description and spiritual interpretation of Rowlandson's experiences (Burnham 1993: 61). She cites Kathryn Zabelle Dorouni-an's categories of 'empirical narration' – a 'colloquial' tone, in which Rowlandson participates in what she describes; and a 'rhetorical narra-tion' – a 'biblical' style, in which Rowlandson's role is that of observer and commentator – and suggests that the split might be characterised as one between Rowlandson's psychological and religious interpreta-tions of her experience (1993: 61). Finally, it is important to distinguish between Rowlandson's claims that she was comforted (as she claims) by certain biblical passages in the immediate moment of her traumatic experiences, and her application of biblical passages to her experiences after the fact, at the time of writing (1993: 21), because this further complicates the idea of the 'curious split'. What *can* be said is that the scriptural references raise another important property of autobiography, pertaining to the distinction between the self who writes the autobio-graphy and the self written about in the autobiography. This is a highly difficult relationship, and one which has to be considered anew when encountering any autobiographical text.

The biblical passage above illustrates these ambiguities: 'See now that I, even I am he, and there is no god with me; I kill and I make alive, I wound and I heal, neither is there any can deliver out of my hand'. Is this Rowlandson's claim to God-like power, obviously not reflective of the ideals of female or Puritan modesty, which the text supposedly endorses? Does the passage signal that Rowlandson feels righteous, destructive, punishing anger towards her captors, her text functioning as a tool of destruction, triumphantly confirming the rightness of Puritan values and God's sanction of them? But boundaries between self and other, life and death, injury and healing are laid waste in this passage (and by Rowlandson's appropriation of it), so that, ultimately, this passage reveals the difficulty of making distinctions, necessary for acts of reading and interpretation, and for the inscription of the rightness of the Puritan worldview. Here may lie the radical potential of Rowlandson's text, in that, as Burnham argues, it reveals Puritan values to be only one of many possible worldviews (1993: 64), one that is, in fact, constructed in relation to other worldviews (1993: 65). This means that Rowlandson's work makes no proprietary, definitive claim to meaning-making (and, by extension, perhaps it lays no colonial claim to dominate and possess the world it describes). It, ultimately, privileges no single reading (it cannot be read as a clear endorsement or demonstration of the correctness of Puritan values). As such, it entertains a world of plurality and multiplicity. That resistance to a single, definitive interpretation of her experiences may be the legacy of Rowlandson's experience in captivity and her subtle challenge to her Puritan community and its values (perhaps especially as they pertain to gender).

Rowlandson should be considered as an individual pulled by the various claims made on her by her community, who both capitulates to, and resists, those claims. Burnham claims that Rowlandson 'occupies a hinge that divides one cultural subjectivity from another, for during her captivity she belongs neither to the Puritan nor to the Indian cultural system' (1993: 64). Her narrative represents various oscillations and equivocations, resulting in an autobiography which dramatises the self and its allegiances as shifting territory. The spatial metaphor here is deliberate, influenced by Logan's focus on this autobiography as a search for 'place' – a reading, in turn, influenced by Rowlandson's decision to structure and punctuate her narrative according to the various 'removes' she undergoes throughout her captivity. Logan rightly notes that 'literal and figurative places overlap' throughout Rowlandson's narrative and that Rowlandson's narrative is about 'the different places Rowlandson occupies and about finding a place to speak' (1993: 256). If Rowlandson speaks from many different places, does her voice and identity also change?

Burnham notes that 'prior to her captivity, the Indian culture did not exist for Rowlandson and her readers other than in the form of a typological symbol' and that Rowlandson's experience, and the written narrative of that experience, 'documents the extraordinary interaction between two cultures that had long inhabited the same country but experienced little contact, especially on such an intimate level and over such an extended period of time' (1993: 61). Rowlandson's text is a transnational autobiography, in that her engagement with her Native American captors illuminates Doyle's emphasis on 'radically co-formed nations, arising from material and ideological forces that continuously transform the existence of both or all national sides' (2009: 1). A co-formed subject, then, Rowlandson's autobiography's oscillations and ambiguities reveal not an anchored identity, but one which is continually transformed and transforming. The self-description in Rowlandson's autobiography does not constitute the act of 'taking home' an 'externally given account of a self'. That is, it does not document the 'happy acquisition' of an identity as 'Puritan'. This is because it is unclear what Rowlandson might understand as 'home', and it is unclear just how her relation to 'home' affects her relationship to that 'externally given account'.

The exemplary 'I' in Benjamin Franklin's *Autobiography* is offered as a secular model of what it might mean to be an American. Born in Boston in 1706, Franklin moved to Philadelphia at the age of 17. He worked as a printer, was responsible for inaugurating a great many civic projects in Philadelphia, and was a member of the committee which drafted the Declaration of Independence. Banes argues that 'the spiritual autobiographer located values through introspection and intuition; the secular autobiographer defined his values by observing the results of his actions. In both cases, the exemplary self emphasises universal principles, while diminishing an individual's importance' (1982: 227). Franklin's narrative proves and disproves this claim. As with Rowlandson's text, the exemplary model of selfhood in Franklin's text is constructed and offered in relation to traumatic cultural events; Franklin's autobiography was written between 1771 and 1790, during and after the period of the American Revolution, when questions of national identity were vital, if uncertain. His text, like Rowlandson's, responds to a perceived desire for an individual who can be representative of a group, thus addressing a need for unity and for a model American citizen exemplifying common, sanctioned values (Banes' 'universal principles'). A record of the public life of a self-made man, Franklin's text offers observations of the results of his actions. But it is difficult to understand Franklin's narrative as attempting to diminish the importance of its writer; it is, rather, the construction and promotion of a particular kind of self which is one of its main achievements.

Perhaps the most obvious indicator that the exemplary self is being understood in the context of a secular framework is revealed in Franklin's focus on 'Errata' ([1771–1790] 2008: 22). Franklin's use of this word shows that he conceives of self-development and identity formation as necessarily entailing mistakes (individuals have faults and failings), but mistakes which can be fixed. Optimistically, he believes that misfortune and misjudgement can be reversed, redressed. In comparison to the more grievous 'sin', implying judgment and punishment from a higher authority, 'errata' places responsibility and the ability to change in the hands of the individual, making a large claim for the potential of self-determination (appealing to citizens of a new nation constructed from revolution). 'Errata' is rooted in Franklin's biographical experience – specifically, his various employments as printer and publisher in Boston, London and Philadelphia. By invoking errata as trope, he converts biographical details of his life into organising, edifying metaphor. This is a secularised version of Rowlandson's practice of typology. While it provides a similar allegorising function, in order to achieve synthesis of personal and national histories, Franklin's is a radical gesture, marking a significant departure from Rowlandson's text and other examples of spiritual autobiography. Franklin locates 'promise' not in God, but in the American citizen, in his ability to fashion (and re-fashion) his identity, to be self-made. Finally, the trope of 'errata' points to another vitally important property of autobiography. Franklin not only offers himself as a model 'fit to be imitated' ([1771–1790] 2008: 3), but as a text to be read – a life lived is equivalent to an edition of a book. This raises questions. Does an autobiography somehow stand in for the writer? Does the text, rather, represent a *part* of the writer and part of the life?

Franklin writes his life at a series of temporal removes. His autobiography exists in four parts; the first part written in 1771, before the Revolutionary War, the second part written 13 years later, parts three and four written more than four years after the second (Shurr 1992: 436–8).

The process of composition is piecemeal. While Franklin did intend these personal writings to be published, William Shurr notes that: 'In fact, there exists no version of the *Autobiography* approved by Franklin himself. Even the title, "Autobiography", is a word that Franklin never used and probably never even heard' (1992: 435). The retrospective labelling of texts as 'autobiography' is a reminder that the history of autobiographical criticism has, in many ways, been a colonising enterprise, involving the co-opting of texts and subjects, and, of course, its early examples are written by colonial (often colonised) subjects.

Franklin's autobiography begins by suggesting that the text is private, for Franklin's son and descendants only:

Dear Son,

I have ever had a Pleasure in obtaining any little Anecdotes of my Ancestors. You may remember the Enquiries I made among the Remains of my Relations when you were with me in England; and the Journey I took for that purpose. Now imagining it may be equally agreable [sic] to you to know the Circumstances of *my* Life, many of which you are yet unacquainted with; and expecting a Weeks uninterrupted Leisure in my present Country Retirement, I sit down to write them for you. To which I have besides some other Inducements. Having emerg'd from the Poverty & Obscurity in which I was born & bred, to a State of Affluence and some Degree of Reputation in the World, and having gone so far thro' Life with a considerable Share of Felicity, the conducing Means I made use of, which, with the Blessing of God, so well succeeded, my Posterity may like to know, as they may find some of them Suitable to their own situations, & therefore fit to be imitated. –That Felicity, when I reflected on it, has induc'd me sometimes to say, that were it offer'd to my Choice, I should have no Objection to a Repetition of the same Life from its Beginning, only asking the Advantages Authors have in a second Edition to correct some Faults of the first. So would I if I might, besides corr the Faults, change some sinister Accidents & Events of it for others more favourable, but tho' this were deny'd, I should still accept the Offer. However, since such a Repetition is not to be expected, the Thing most like Living one's life over again, seems to be a *Recollection* of that Life; and to make that Recollection as durable as possible, the putting it down in Writing. ([1771–1790] 2008: 3–4)

The first part of Franklin's autobiography may constitute an effort to amend 'errata' concerning his familial relations; the son, William, is illegitimate. His autobiography could be read as striving towards reparation and compensation – restoration. However, as Shurr explains, Franklin's son would have been in his forties at the time of writing, so it is doubtful that he would require advice from his father (1992: 440). This renders Franklin's intention, and the intended readership for his text, uncertain. Christopher Looby argues, convincingly, that the paternal role Franklin invokes in the first part of the autobiography allows him to situate himself as a (founding) father figure for the nation and its citizens, his future descendants (hence, the emphasis on 'posterity') (Looby 1986: 73). This is additionally supported by the second part of the *Autobiography*, which is prefaced by two letters, urging Franklin to make his life story public for others. The letters provide Franklin's self-justificatory explanation and one 'autobiographical occasion' – here, offered to alleviate concerns that the autobiographer is motivated by self-interest. The inclusion of the letters serves as a playful, explicit illustration of Franklin's capacities for dexterous strategising (political, literary) and opportunism – skills which served him well throughout his career and are necessary to the acts of self-publicising undertaken in his autobiography. If Banes is correct in arguing that 'autobiography combines another kind of synthesis; this time, of the "memoir" (public record of a life) and "confession" (private reflection)' (1982: 226), then the inclusion of the letters also functions to usher autobiography from the realm of the private ('Dear Son') into that of the public.

Benjamin Vaughan's letter informs Franklin that: '"All that has happened to you is also connected with the detail of the manners and situation of *a rising* people"' (74). This argument makes clear what Jennifer Jordan Baker calls the 'presumption of representativeness in the text' (2000: 274). That is, Franklin's life history is understood by himself, and others, as emblematic of the American experience. As in Rowlandson's text, but for different reasons, this exemplary status is problematic. Embracing this reading of Franklin as representative, James M. Cox argues that Franklin:

> dates the time of his writing so that the dates of composition [...] are not biographical information but textual reality. Thus the 'life', which is to say Franklin's account of his early years, is placed within the years 1771–1778, the years of the American Revolution, confederation, and

constitution. What literally happens in the form of Franklin's work is that the history of the revolution, in which Franklin played such a conspicuous part, is displaced by the narrative of Franklin's early life, so that Franklin's personal history *stands in place of the revolution*. [...] But this represented history was not the actual revolution. There still remained the form which would realise the revolution and thus stand for it. That form was the autobiography – the life of a self-made, self-governing man written by the man himself. (1971: 258–9)

Cox does not consider the full implications of his argument, especially as they pertain to the political and ethical consequences of the structural and topical displacement he outlines and the conclusion he draws: that autobiography is the genre suited to representing America. For Cox, Franklin's personal history and autobiographical form somehow stand in for the Revolution. In making himself – an individual – representative of a nation, Franklin can be understood as belonging to the category of 'representative men', as described by Emerson in essays published in 1850, whose life story is emblematic of the culture in which he participates. But Franklin can be representative only, and precisely, because he displaces (stands in for) other complex histories. His claim to representative status is facilitated by the fact that his gendered and racial identities are properties designating him as belonging to his culture's most highly valued identity groups. In Berlant's terms, Franklin installs himself as the 'constitutional American "person"', because he *is* one – the white male property owner. The case for Franklin's representative status, made by Franklin and many of his subsequent readers and critics, like Cox, excludes the experiences and voices of those whom Franklin cannot represent, those refused the 'fantasy of national democracy' (Berlant 1997: 18–19) and who, by implication, might not be able to lay claim to an identity as 'American'.

Looby claims that Franklin's autobiography contains:

certain traces of the revolutionary conflict, but also (and more significantly) certain traces of Franklin's deeply felt wish to defer the Revolution. That is, the first part of his text, written in 1771, expresses this desire; the subsequent parts, the writing of which he deferred until after the Revolution had taken place, express his misgivings with respect to the revolutionary struggle and his desire to repress the memory of it in the interest of ensuring a return to social and political order. (1986: 72)

Looby's argument that Franklin's autobiography functions to *defer*, not stand in for, the Revolution must be considered in relation to Cox's reading and also in relation to one of the most important strategies of the text. As a means of illustrating and proving his representative status, Franklin offers himself to readers as a gift – explicitly, as a model 'fit to be imitated'. In the second part of the *Autobiography*, he describes how he 'conceiv'd the bold and arduous Project of arriving at moral Perfection' ([1771–1790] 2008: 84). To this end, and for readers' edification, he offers a list and description of the virtues he believes to be important and discussion of his own attempts to cultivate those virtues, including a sample from a book, in which he dedicates a page to each virtue, summarising his progress (84–9). Three aspects of this gesture are striking. Firstly, Franklin's focus on moral perfection occupies as important a role in his text as his pursuit of material success – in fact, he argues that it is through the exercise of virtue that worldly success can be achieved. A problem with this logic, of course, is the implication that material failure is personal failure, so that Franklin's text encapsulates the problems, contradictions and paradoxes of the American Dream. Secondly, Franklin's pursuit of moral perfection reveals that his writing is indebted to the conventions of spiritual autobiography (his 'anecdotes' often take the form of parables, for example, and he is fond of maxims), even as it is thoroughly self-interested. Thirdly, and most intriguingly, autobiographical writing (the sample page from his book of virtues) appears within Franklin's *Autobiography* itself, offered as a means towards achieving self-development. Franklin's gesture of offering the self to the reader as a model to be emulated, together with the proffering of autobiographical writing within an autobiographical text as a tool to aid personal development, exemplifies a faith in the power of autobiography to effect social change – a faith which can be found in many subsequent autobiographies.

However, the motives for, and consequences of, this gesture of offering the self as a model for others must be considered, along with the purposes to which autobiographical writings are put. Leigh Gilmore provides an excellent summary of the relationship between autobiography and the problem of representativeness (the self as exemplary):

American individualism is informed by a democratic ideology of *e pluribus unum*. Stand up, it says, and represent yourself. Or, sit back and designate someone else to represent you. This intertwining of individual and collective representation demonstrates the close relation between representing yourself and participating in a representative structure in which one may stand for many. There is a long tradition in autobiography of representing the self as utterly unique and, on precisely this basis, able to stand for others through acts of self-inspection and self-revelation. (2001: 19)

Franklin's text stands as an early, and particularly notable, example of the means by which, in Gilmore's terms, 'autobiography helps to install a sovereign subject' (2001: 21). If Franklin's text defers the Revolution, its incitement of readers to be like him might, nonetheless, be read as a (politically motivated) effort to influence the construction of the American citizen in the future – as one who, ironically, will displace or defer the political with the personal, who will prioritise the individual over the relational, sameness over difference. The 'long tradition' in autobiography that Gilmore refers to, above, is that of the 'representative man': the rational, enlightened subject who speaks for himself and is constructed by himself and others as capable of speaking for others. But what of those who cannot imitate Franklin? In Franklin's text, the freedoms and privileges of white male identity comprise the model to be emulated. Franklin's encouragement of readers to follow his example and advice is, therefore, far from altruistic. Fantasising about the opportunity to live his life over again, Franklin nevertheless admits that 'such a repetition is not to be expected' ([1771–1790] 2008: 4). Nonetheless, his desire appears to be that other Americans live his life over again. And by offering himself as a gift to others – a model to be emulated – Franklin objectifies himself. By so doing, he confirms Laura Marcus's claim that 'the "self" as capital or property is essential to the newly emergent bourgeoise' (1994: 16), who, in Felicity Nussbaum's terms, 'formed a class that would begin to keep an unprecedented record of its individual selves' (1989: 16). By offering himself as gift, as model, Franklin converts the self into capital, as valuable property.

Matthew Peters observes a tendency in criticism on American autobiography from the 1970s onwards to argue that 'the American autobiography was a revolutionary genre' (2005: 241). This point cannot be dismissed. It may partly explain why autobiographies have *always* generated (or courted) judgment, censure and controversy – another factor necessitating the frequent inclusion of the author's self-justificatory explanation for writing. However, such claims tend to echo Parini's claims about American identity and are based on analysis of a select few autobiographers – Franklin, in particular. Clearly, not all revolutionary autobiographies are American, and Peters' claim that 'it is useful to think of an American autobiography as standing outside an American tradition as it is to identify American characteristics within it' (2005: 241) is particularly productive. This can be seen by examining *The Interesting Narrative of the Life of Olaudah Equiano, or Gustavus Vassa, the African. Written by Himself* (1789). This text is notable, not because it is revolutionary (although it is), but because the revolution comprises an attempt to lay claim to the sovereign subject which autobiography can install, but which its writer has been denied. Equiano's autobiography constitutes a passionate and eloquent (if occasionally ambivalent) protestation against the institution of slavery. It describes his birth in Nigeria, his enslavement (he is sold to English slave traders, transported to the West Indies) and the eventual purchase of his freedom in 1766. In the centuries following its publication, the text has provoked major critical debates regarding Equiano's identity, his attitudes to slavery and the truthfulness of its famous description of the Middle Passage, something with implications for its status as autobiography.

The opening paragraph of the *Interesting Narrative* is suggestive in explaining why Equiano's text has generated the interpretive difficulties described above:

> I believe it is difficult for those who publish their own memoirs to escape the imputation of vanity; nor is this the only disadvantage under which they labour; it is also their misfortune, that whatever is uncommon is rarely, if ever, believed; and what is obvious we are apt to turn from with disgust, and to charge the writer with impertinence. People generally think those memoirs only worthy to be read or remembered which abound in great or striking events; those, in short, which in a high degree excite either admiration or pity: all others they consign to contempt and oblivion. It is, therefore, I confess, not a little hazardous, in a private and obscure individual, and a stranger too, thus to solicit the indulgent attention of the public; especially when I own I offer here the history of neither a saint, a hero, nor a tyrant. I believe there are a few events in my life which have not happened to many; it is true the incidents of it are numerous; and, did I consider myself an European, I might say my sufferings were great; but, when I compare my lot with that of most of my countrymen, I regard myself as a *particular favourite of Heaven*, and acknowledge the mercies of Providence in every occurrence of my life. If, then, the following narrative does not appear sufficiently interesting to engage general attention,

let my motive be some excuse for its publication. I am not so foolishly vain as to expect from it either immortality or literary reputation. If it affords any satisfaction to my numerous friends, at whose request it has been written, or in the smallest degree promotes the interest of humanity, the ends for which it was undertaken will be fully attained, and every wish of my heart gratified. Let it therefore be remembered that, in wishing to avoid censure, I do not aspire to praise. ([1789] 2003: 31–2)

Equiano has a nuanced appreciation of the difficulties and hazards of his project, and his text begins by attempting to anticipate or diminish them. Political and cultural imperatives force him to undertake a series of careful equivocations, which ensure that neither his identity nor his values are stated explicitly. What is clear, though, is that he claims the right to speak, write and be heard in a Western culture which does not grant him subject status, whether he is a slave (his owner's property, object rather than subject) or not (a free man, but a former slave, living in a world which regards him as inferior). Unlike Rowlandson and Franklin, who write largely for readers in communities to which they already belong, however fragile that sense of belonging, Equiano cannot assume that his (predominantly white) readers will be receptive, sympathetic or respectful towards him. He must earn readers' trust and favour, and he attempts to do this by conforming to, and meeting, white standards of value. His narrative is legitimated by the lengthy list of individuals which prefaces the text (15–28), acknowledging the subscriptions enabling the book to be published. Equiano is dependent upon the white establishment to facilitate the publication of his text, to confer upon him the authority to speak, to authenticate what he says as truth.

And yet, the aim of his text is to protest against the values shared by many of his readers. Bart Moore-Gilbert argues that Equiano's text enlists autobiography 'to advance the reclamation of personhood deformed by colonialism' (2009: 7). This complex act of 'reclamation', not unlike the problematic term 'restoration' in Rowlandson's narrative, suggests both that Equiano wishes to write himself back to an originary condition, untainted by the experience of slavery (he notes that: 'I still look back with pleasure on the first scenes of my life, though that pleasure has been for the most part mingled with sorrow' ([1789] 2003: 46)), and that he writes to claim a degree of autonomy and value which he has never, hitherto, enjoyed. Equiano's precarious position, in relation to his readers, places limitations on the explicitness of his protestation against slavery and necessitates extreme care in making pronouncements and declarations relating to his self-presentation. As a result, such statements tend to be implicit, ambiguous – 'did I consider myself an European', and references to 'my countrymen' are circumspect, non-committal. Equiano's narrative voice, like Rowlandson's, performs numerous oscillations. He shifts from expressing identification with his readers ('what is obvious we are apt to turn from in disgust') and differentiating himself from them ('I believe there are a few incidents in my life which have not happened to many'). He elevates himself as exceptional ('I regard myself as a *particular favourite of Heaven*'), yet simultaneously claims no credit for his achievements ('I offer here the history of neither a saint, a hero, nor a tyrant'). Like Rowlandson and Franklin, he claims to write at the urging of others. The political intent of Equiano's narrative is signalled by the use of the word 'interest', which appears twice in this opening paragraph. The first instance of the word occurs within the context of Equiano's modest hope that his narrative will satisfy readers' curiosity: 'If, then, the following narrative does not appear sufficiently interesting to engage general attention, let my motive be some excuse for its publication'. Eve Sedgwick's discussion of shame in the work of Silvan Tomkins, in relation to Henry James' depression and writings, is helpful in explaining how 'interest' is central to Equiano's autobiographical project:

> As Tomkins writes, 'Like disgust, [shame] operates only after interest or enjoyment has been activated, and inhibits one or the other or both. The innate activator of shame is the incomplete reduction of interest or joy. Hence any barrier to further exploration which partially reduces interest ... will activate the lowering of the head and eyes in shame and reduce further exploration or self-exposure' (*Shame* 135). To consider interest itself a distinct affect and to posit an association between shame and (the [incomplete] inhibition of) interest makes sense phenomenogically [sic], I think [...]. (2003: 39)

The relationship between interest and shame outlined here makes it conceivable that Equiano wishes readers to find his narrative 'interesting', only to the extent that their 'interest' in his story is then to be inhibited by the text's determination to induce shame, regarding their possible complicity in, or tolerance of, the institution of slavery. The implication that 'some excuse' is needed for publication of the text also suggests that autobiography, the project of self-presentation, may inspire shame on the part of the autobiographer. Surely, this is another reason for the apologetic or defensive justifications for writing (the insistence on specifying the text's 'autobiographical occasion'), which so many autobiographies contain, and it might explain autobiographers' frequent insistence that they write not for self-interest, but for the benefit of others. And, surely, complex relations of interest and shame are integral to the 'productive alienation' described by Riley as necessary to acts of self-description, which, this chapter argues, are a central task of autobiography.

The second instance of the word 'interest' subtly advances the political intent of Equiano's narrative, which is designed to educate readers about the inhumanities of slavery and, in doing so, assist in changing the attitudes of some and the plight of others: 'If it affords any satisfaction to my numerous friends, at whose request it has been written, or in the smallest degree promotes the interest of humanity, the ends for which it was undertaken will be fully attained, and every wish of my heart gratified' ([1789] 2003: 31–2). Equiano suggests that Enlightenment values (such as reason and truth) and goals (production of the sovereign, rational subject, the equality of democracy) are faultily thought and illogically applied; humanity's 'interest' will not be improved if subject status – personhood – is given to some individuals, but refused to others. This is a radical political statement, especially because Equiano does not wait for others to grant him subject status. He claims it for himself; he claims it while emphasising a self-description as 'African', and he shows this by writing autobiography – a form of writing which treats the development of the Enlightenment subject (usually figured as white, European). That is to say, writing autobiography is one means of facilitating Equiano's act of 'moving towards and accepting some externally given account of a self' (Riley 2000: 2) – an account which he not only accepts, but revises.

Missing from Equiano's opening passage is the word 'truth'. That Equiano's narrative is intended to be read as truth is signalled by the words 'memoirs', 'history' and the statement that he recounts events of his life. Yet, the truthfulness of elements of Equiano's text are contentious, following Vince Carretta's discovery of baptismal records, suggesting that Equiano may have been born in South Carolina, not Africa, as he claims (Carretta, in Firsch 2007: 46). Equiano's description of his African origins and account of the Middle Passage may, therefore, be fictive. Carretta speculates that Equiano may have 'invented rather than reclaimed an African identity' (Firsch 2007: 46), in order to speak on behalf of others who were enslaved. He offers a sympathetic reading of Equiano's motives for, possibly, fabricating his identity. Paradoxically, this reading relies on understanding the text as autobiography (supposedly, a truthful record of a life):

> Every autobiography is an act of re-creation, and autobiographers are not under oath when they are reconstructing their lives. Furthermore, an autobiography is an act of rhetoric. That is, any autobiography is designed to influence a reader's impression of its author, and often, as in the case of the *Interesting Narrative*, to affect the reader's beliefs or actions as well. No autobiographer has faced a greater opportunity for redefinition than has a manumitted (freed) slave. (2007: 46)

This reading is problematic for many reasons. The most important concerns its evasion of the fact that, for many readers, autobiographers *are* under an oath of sorts, because autobiography implies a promise to tell the truth. Cathy Davidson lists other problems which this reading fails to solve:

> Is Equiano/Vassa [...] one of the only victims of the heinous Middle Passage to write about it? Or was Equiano/Vassa actually an ex-slave from South Carolina who invented the Middle Passage sequence in *The Interesting Narrative* from other sources and from his own imagination, thus making him author of a compelling and genre-defining slave narrative that was, at its foundation, fictional? If it turns out that Equiano/Vassa was born in South Carolina, does that change the literary significance of *The Interesting Narrative* as a literary text and a historical document? How and to what extent? If Equiano/Vassa is a liar, should we still be teaching him, or is *The Interesting Narrative* simply a hoax that deserves to be disregarded? (Davidson 2006/2007: 25)

The problem of determining the truth-status of the Middle Passage description, in particular, is oddly analogous to the problem of assessing what happens to the American Revolution in Franklin's *Narrative*. In Franklin's text, the question pertains to the absence of an important historical event. Where is the Revolution – displaced or deferred? In Equiano's text, the question is whether the inclusion of a historical event (the Middle Passage experience) is truthful or not (if it is not truthful, perhaps it should not have been included)? Whereas Franklin's displacement or deferral privileges his personal history, Equiano's inclusion of the Middle Passage description may well function to foreground the voices and experiences of others – a gesture which compromises the truth-status of his text and renders it problematic as autobiography. Nonetheless, Equiano's motives for including this description may well be less self-interested, if more risky, than Franklin's act of displacement. Rather than concluding that Equiano is a 'liar' who concocts a hoax, a generous reading of his text might conclude that his inclusion of the Middle Passage description tests what autobiography is and can do. Moore-Gilbert argues that Equiano 'contravenes one of the primary strategies of traditional spiritual autobiography, the attainment of unity of personhood' (2009: 11). Instead, as the inclusion of the Middle Passage experience suggests, he proffers a model of selfhood which is relational, fragmented and multiple and which may well be a fiction; all of this de-centres the value and privilege attached to the Western Enlightenment subject, as well as questioning what is meant by one of its most important concepts: truth. As Laura Doyle argues: 'Equiano is fully aware that his position is a transnational one in which he mediates among a network of racialised national players and traditions – all within an Atlantic theater of battles, betrayal, profiteering, and rape, as well as solidarity, ethical agency, and generosity' (2009: 16).

Equiano's *Interesting Narrative* is often credited as an important influence on the nineteenth century American slave narrative. Audrey Firsch notes that Equiano and his autobiography are 'pivotal to the interplay between the slave narrative and abolition' (2007: 2). The slave narrative has a crucially important place in the history of American autobiography, although it was only in the mid- to late twentieth century, and partly due to the political influence of the Civil Rights' movements of the 1960s, that the importance and the value of slave narratives were widely recognised (2007: 1). The label, 'slave narrative', itself is something of a misnomer. *Not* being a slave is central to the slave narrative, as such narratives were written by former (freed or escaped) slaves. They recount the horrific details of enslaved existence and record the process by which an enslaved self becomes free, as a crucial means by which to convey a central argument – that the institution of slavery be abolished. An identity as 'ex' or 'former' slave conferred a degree of safety, however small, while acknowledging the direct experience of slavery necessary to make such narratives powerfully authentic. Writing as a former slave enabled the autobiographer to speak with authority about the experience of slavery, to critique the institution from outwith its bounds. This situation also renders highly visible a particular difficulty for autobiography: that of the relationship between the 'I' writing the autobiography and the 'I' written about within its pages. This relationship might also be considered as one of 'productive alienation'. As Carretta notes: '[t]he profoundest possible transformation is the one any slave underwent when freed, moving from the legal status of property to that of person, from commodity to human being' (Carretta, in Firsch 2007: 47).

Slave narratives reveal many important properties of autobiographies (perhaps American autobiographies, in particular). They reveal two central aims of autobiography: to give voice to the disenfranchised and to effect political change. The slave narrative also exposes tensions central to many autobiographies. The conundrum of representation is central to autobiography. It forces consideration of the relationships between individual and group identity enacted or negotiated in any particular text. Other than him or herself, who is the autobiographer speaking for or on behalf of? If the autobiographer attempts to speak for others, who is excluded or co-opted (colonised?) in the process? If autobiography is to be used to effect political change, then just how might this be achieved? Often, autobiographers write to change the values or minds of their readers; to encourage readers to share the autobiographer's views. Finally, while it is correct to argue that the nineteenth century slave narrative constitutes a particularly 'American' narrative form, addressing the institution of slavery in America and how this institution challenged the principles of democracy, equality and freedom imagined as central to American identity (hence, the pointed subtitle of Douglass' text, 'An American Slave'), it should be remembered that the slave narrative, like the institution of slavery itself, is, by necessity, a transnational genre, rather than an 'American' one, in any circumscribed or exceptionalist sense, because the slave trade was a transnational enterprise. Kerry Sinanan notes how the slave trade (and the slave narrative) reflects 'the cultural exchanges of the black Atlantic between Britain, Africa and America' (Sinanan, in Firsch 2007: 62). The slave narratives of Frederick Douglass and Harriet Jacobs are often considered as exemplary, because of their engagement with the aims and tensions described above. Gender emerges as central to each writer's acts of self-presentation, their political agendas and the strategies they invoke, in order to appeal to their audiences.

Frederick Douglass was born in 1818. He spent much of his enslaved life in Baltimore and Maryland, before escaping from Baltimore at the age of 19 and subsequently working for the anti-slavery movement. *Narrative of the Life of Frederick Douglass, An American Slave* (1845) contains a preface written by William Lloyd Garrison, leader of the American Anti-Slavery Society. Its opening contention must be questioned, not to discredit or challenge the status of Douglass' text as autobiography (although Douglass did have to counter many such accusations), but because of what this reveals about Douglass' complex relationship with his audience:

> Mr. DOUGLASS has very properly chosen to write his own Narrative, in his own style, and according to the best of his ability, rather than to employ some one else. It is, therefore, entirely his own production; and, considering how long and dark was the career he had to run as a slave, – how few have been his opportunities to improve his mind since he broke his iron fetters, – it is, in my judgment, highly creditable to his head and heart. He who can pursue it without a tearful eye, a heaving breast, an afflicted spirit, – without being filled with an unutterable abhorrence of slavery and all its abettors, and animated with a determination to seek the immediate overthrow of that execrable system, – without trembling for the fate of this country in the hands of a righteous God, who is ever on the side of the oppressed, and whose arm is not shortened that it cannot save, – must have a flinty heart, and be qualified to act the part of a trafficker 'in slaves and the souls of men.' I am confident that it is essentially true in all its statements; that nothing has been set down in malice, nothing exaggerated, nothing drawn from the imagination; that it comes short of the reality, rather than overstates a single fact in regard to SLAVERY AS IT IS. (Douglass [1845] 2009: 7)

Conventionally, a slave narrative contained a white-authored preface written by an individual with abolitionist sympathies, whose authority legitimated, framed and mediated the slave narrator for a white audience. Douglass' word alone is not enough to confirm the veracity of his account. John Sekora describes this phenomenon as 'Black message/ White envelope' (1987). The necessity of this 'white envelope' emphasises the fact that a slave narrator, like Equiano, addressed an audience which constructed him or her as 'other', thus revealing the magnitude and difficulty of the political aims of slave narratives. In his role as legitimiser, Garrison decides that Douglass is 'proper' – his story fit for a white audience to read. Garrison's aim is to convince readers that Douglass is civilised and cultivated – attributes withheld from African-Americans in the nineteenth century, white, cultural imagination. Douglass' dependence on white authority also suggests that the freedom Douglass enjoys as a former slave is not unqualified. Indeed, John Stauffer argues that when giving speeches, Douglass was introduced to audiences by abolitionist organisers 'as a piece of property, a thing, an it' (Stauffer, in Lee 2009: 18). It is because of this dependence on white authority and approval, and the fact that Douglass' narrative (even his person) was used for the purposes of others, that any claim that Douglass's narrative is 'his own' must be treated with caution.

What Douglass deems proper and what Garrison deems proper is not necessarily the same thing. This is a tension pertinent to the slave narrative in general and, arguably, to consideration of any autobiography written by a disenfranchised or subordinated individual, who addresses readers who may be responsible for that subordination or who shares the values which facilitate it. How can Douglass ensure that his text advances the purposes he wishes it to serve, without it being co-opted by the interests of others? Specifically, how can he convince a white readership of the necessity of abolishing slavery, when slavery is an experience white readers will never experience? Douglass attempts to convince his audience of the necessity of abolishing slavery by showing the weak and insubstantial nature of the arguments made to justify slavery and by including emotive, sensational and sentimental episodes designed to affect a reader. For example, his narrative famously opens with his recollection of a childhood memory of a female slave being beaten by her master, undercutting the belief that slave owners functioned as benevolent paternal figures towards their slaves ([1845] 2009: 19). He also shows the absurdity of understanding the plantation as an Edenic place, where slaves lived happily, making the un-Christian nature of slavery abundantly clear, contrary to the protestations of those who defended the practice ([1845] 2009: 74). As Garrison says, Douglass appeals to the 'head and the heart' of his audience, participating in Enlightenment philosophical debates about reason and the passions predominant in the eighteenth and nineteenth centuries. But Garrison's patronage of Douglass extends to suggesting how readers should respond to the text: with tears and strong emotion. Garrison's insistence that Douglass' narrative reveals '[s]lavery as it is' is disingenuous. His preface, including its advice on how to respond to the text, screens readers from the 'reality' of the experience of slavery. Garrison's preface is notable for its failure to suggest strategies readers could pursue to further the abolitionist cause – it emphasises that audiences should feel, rather than act. That reason was privileged over sentiment, and sentiment often 'feminised', makes Garrison's advice even more problematic. Whether these are the sole responses Douglass would have desired from his audience seems doubtful. His text endorses law-breaking and violence as one means to achieving the end of slavery, emblematised by the incident in which Douglass asserts his independence from Covey: 'You have seen how a man was made a slave; you shall see how a slave was made a man' ([1845] 2009: 63).

Douglass' advocacy of action in the form of violence problematises his twin desires to speak for himself and to speak on behalf of a wider group (the issue of representation is problematic for him). An identity as 'man' is one in which his identity as a slave jeopardises, but an identity as 'man' is a vital part of Douglass' self-description. However, advocating violence as a means of *group* action (for other slaves to be made men) could trouble his reception by a white readership. Douglass' valorisation of manliness, demonstrated and achieved via violence, additionally raises questions about who he speaks for. That he wishes to speak for the experiences of other former and currently enslaved individuals appears clear:

> I now come to that part of my life during which I planned, and finally succeeded in making, my escape from slavery. But before narrating any of the peculiar circumstances, I deem it proper to make known my intention not to state all the facts connected with the transaction. My reasons for pursuing this course may be understood from the following: First, were I to give a minute statement of all the facts, it is not only possible, but quite probable, that others would thereby be involved in the most embarrassing difficulties. Secondly, such a statement would most undoubtedly induce greater vigilance on the part of slaveholders than has existed heretofore among them; which would, of course, be the means of guarding a door whereby some dear brother bondman might escape his galling chains. ([1845] 2009: 88)

Douglass withholds information so that he does not make it difficult for 'others' to escape. However, it is doubtful whether he takes the experiences of female slaves into consideration ('some dear brother bondsman'). Deborah McDowell has written about the numerous scenes of violence in the *Narrative*, in which women function as victims, in ways designed to stimulate concern and outrage on the part of a white audience. She notes that these voyeuristic scenes also serve to titillate audiences, by eroticising subjugation and punishment (McDowell 1999, in Douglass [1845] 2009: xxi). In Douglass' narrative, she argues, male slaves attempt to counter their position as victims (and emphasise that they are men), by using violence and resisting being whipped, whereas women are not given this option (1999, in Douglass [1845] 2009: xx). The fact that Douglass achieves freedom partly due to the assistance of his future wife, for example, is not emphasised, and Stauffer notes that 'much like the other classic male "I" narratives of the era, from Melville's *Moby-Dick* and Thoreau's *Walden* to Whitman's *Leaves of Grass*, self-transformation and emancipation came at the expense of family and domestic life, and the role of husband' (Stauffer, in Firsch 2007: 214). While Douglass' public sympathy towards female enfranchisement is clear in his speeches (McDowell 1999, in Douglass [1845] 2009: xv), sympathy and advocacy on behalf of women's experiences is not apparent in this – his earliest and most famous autobiographical work.

In Douglass' case, and in relation to this text, this is understandable. Robert S. Levine notes the centrality of Franklin's text in the history of autobiography and its influence on the slave narrative. In particular, Levine argues that the

> linking of the autobiographical self with the founding revolutionary ideals of the new nation would be central to the numerous slave narratives that drew on key aspects of Franklin's autobiography: the emphasis on the self-made life, the value of capitalist exchange and possessive individualism in the creation of a 'free self'; the strategic uses of rhetoric, literacy, and deception in a competitive social landscape; and the importance of linking the self to the larger ideals of the community. Slave narrators vary in their responses to Franklin, placing different emphases on different aspects of this 'American' model and in some cases challenging and subverting the model. (Levine, in Firsch 2007: 102–3)

As if he is a reader who accepts Franklin's gift of himself as a model 'fit to be imitated', Douglass shows readers that a former slave can meet (white) American standards of civilisation and success. But Douglass perpetuates the gendered bias ingrained in those white standards.

Douglass also counters pro-slavery arguments with irony and humour, and in his understanding of the importance of reason and sentiment, action and affect function as a political tool in his narrative:

I did not, when a slave, understand the deep meaning of those rude and apparently incoherent songs. I was myself within the circle; so that I neither saw nor heard as those without might see and hear. They told a tale of woe which was then altogether beyond my feeble comprehension; they were tones loud, long, and deep; they breathed the prayer and complaint of souls boiling over with the bitterest anguish. Every tone was a testimony against slavery, and a prayer to God for deliverance from chains. The hearing of those wild notes always depressed my spirit, and filled me with ineffable sadness. I have frequently found myself in tears while hearing them. The mere recurrence to those songs, even now, afflicts me; and while I am writing these lines, an expression of feeling has already found its way down my cheek. ([1845] 2009: 24)

The rhetorical skills displayed here reinforce Douglass' claim that the acquisition of literacy is 'the pathway from slavery to freedom' ([1845] 2009: 39). In this passage, though, the acquisition of literacy arguably functions not only to provide continuity between the 'I' narrated and the 'I' who narrates, but also enables the conversion from 'I' narrated (slave) to 'I' narrating (free). The ability to be affected by the memory of songs as he writes his autobiography (in effect, his text appeals to his own heart) makes it clear that, in many ways, Douglass is still 'within the circle', even as his text and its political aims are (only?) made possible by his ability to describe the experience of slavery as one, and for those, 'without'.

Critics examining autobiographies by women often begin their analyses by observing that women have found it less likely that their voices will be perceived as truthful. Leigh Gilmore explains why this is so:

Much autobiography criticism acknowledges an interpretive division between those who take autobiography as a factual document and those who view it as much more closely, and less damningly, aligned with fiction. This very division, however, results from premises about autobiography's relation to 'truth' in conjunction with premises about the 'truthful' and 'authentic' subject position that autobiography itself constructs. The ethical and political meanings of this subject position contain powerful contradictions: whereas 'truth' is the neutral term toward which all persons strive (this is, by humanist definitions, our task and our reward), some are already farther ahead in the climb and stand to reap more massive material rewards for their efforts, while

others may climb a bit behind or to the side of those persons who are
privileged through their proximity to the alignment of 'truth' with
race, class, gender, and sexual orientation. Some stories are criminal-
ised from the start when the amount of 'truth' one can claim devolves
from the amount of cultural authority already attached, within
a terrain of dominance, to the person speaking and the place from
which s/he speaks. (1994: 25–6)

Gender is central to Harriet Jacobs' *Incidents in the Life of a Slave Girl,
Written by Herself* (1861). The titles of Jacobs' and Douglass' texts bear
out Margo Culley's fascinating observation that:

> American male autobiographers, black and white, inscribe gender on
> the titles of texts much less often than do women (a ratio of one to ten),
> and white American autobiographers, male and female, inscribe race
> in their titles virtually not at all. This is by no means to argue that race
> and gender are not essential elements in the construction of the self
> for members of the dominant culture, but only that race and gender
> are not the necessary categories with which the writer must begin
> when the white and/or male subject takes itself as object of scrutiny.
> We come to understand their priority to every other category only in
> noticing their absence. (1992: 8)

Gender is also a central factor in explaining why Jacobs' text has
only recently gained importance in discussions of the slave narrative.
Stephanie A. Smith notes that it was not until 1987 that the text was
finally authenticated as non-fiction – on publication of the Harvard
University Press edition of the text, edited by Jean Yellin (Smith, in
Firsch 2007: 189). Until that point, the text had most often been categorised (and dismissed) as fiction. Rafia Zafar notes that Jacobs 'had to
contend with a sceptical readership that said her work could not be
"genuine" because of her emphasis on the domestic, her "melodramatic"
style, and her unwillingness to depict herself as an avatar of self-reliance'
(Zafar, in Garfield and Zafar 1996: 4). Jacobs' decision to write under the
pseudonym 'Linda Brent' further troubled the question of determining
whether her text was autobiographical or fictional. While Jacobs shares
with Douglass the difficulties of writing for a white audience, which
has the power to legitimate and judge her (Jacobs' narrative is prefaced
by the white abolitionist, Lydia Maria Childs), the forms of oppression
Jacobs experiences, and her means of resisting and documenting them,
are dictated, to some extent, by her gender.

As discussed, Douglass' text asserts, and convinces readers of, his identity as 'man' (and as 'American', too, perhaps), by inscribing himself within the Franklinian autobiographical model. Jacobs cannot write herself into this paradigm. The nineteenth century cult of True Womanhood envisaged a white woman as embodying its ideal of purity, domesticity, submissiveness and virtue, ensuring that any effort Jacobs might make to challenge the doctrine, or explain why she does not conform to it (both of which she attempts to do in her text), only reinforces the doctrine, by underscoring her exclusion from, and transgression of it. While Jacobs cannot be too explicit about the forms of abuse she suffers and the strategies she employs to resist them, lest this jeopardise her own reputation and offend her readership – imagined as primarily white and female – she does describe the predatory advances of her owner, Dr Flint, and the difficult strategies she must resort to, in order to protect herself (she begins a relationship with another man, in the hope that it will afford her some protection from Flint, and hides in an attic space for seven years).

The opening of Jacobs' narrative confirms Culley's point that, for her, race and gender *are* the 'necessary categories with which the writer must begin':

> I was born a slave; but I never knew it till six years of happy childhood had passed away. My father was a carpenter, and considered so intelligent and skilful in his trade, that, when buildings out of the common line were to be erected, he was sent for from long distances, to be head workman. On condition of paying his mistress two hundred dollars a year, and supporting himself, he was allowed to work at his trade, and manage his own affairs. His strongest wish was to purchase his children; but, though he several times offered his hard earnings for that purpose, he never succeeded. In complexion my parents were a light shade of brownish yellow, and were termed mulattoes. They lived together in a comfortable home; and, though we were all slaves, I was so fondly shielded that I never dreamed I was a piece of merchandise, trusted to them for safe keeping, and liable to be demanded of them at any moment. ([1861] 2000: 7)

While Jacobs cannot give an account of her origins, in the way a reader might expect, the absence of specific details of her birth (she was born in North Carolina, possibly in 1813) is one feature that is common to the slave narrative (Olney 1984: 50). It is also notable for its acknowledgement that familial ties of affection and care protected ('shielded') her; until she becomes aware of the injustices in her society, she is not aware of the difference in her status. The notion of family as shield – as protective, combative device – provides Jacobs with the primary impetus for her subsequent behaviour in adult life, speaking, as it does, particularly to gendered conceptions of women as guardians of moral purity in the domestic sphere. Her autobiographical project makes use of various shielding strategies. For example, Jacobs shields her white female readers from the most graphic details of her abuse. She also shields herself, defending herself against the fact that she has failed to meet her society's standards of ideal (white) female behaviour. Shielding strategies thus enable Jacobs to both question and conform to dominant constructions of female behaviour. The use of the pseudonym is another such strategy; indeed, Zafar explains how it enables Jacobs to 'shield herself from public view' (1996: 12), as it allows her to speak truthfully. The disruption caused by removal of family ties and attachments (that protective shield) is something Jacobs emphasises in her narrative, especially in relation to her difficult relationship with her grandmother, whose judgment of Jacobs' behaviour causes her great distress ([1861] 2000: 63). That disruption heralds Jacobs' understanding of her status as property. Most obviously, Jacobs also feels the desire and duty to shield, or preserve, her family (her two children). This renders flight and escape as invalid options and explains her decision to hide in the attic space – an existence necessitating great physical distress and deprivation, but enabling her to keep watch over her children and extend them some degree of protection and care. In a fascinating analysis, Crispin Sartwell describes the tiny attic space in which Jacobs hides and which she describes as a 'loophole' (1998: 130), in terms which suggest that it can be understood as a further shielding strategy:

> This is her perfect vengeance upon [Dr Flint] though he is unaware of it: she sees him without being seen by him, knows him without being known by him. She ceases to be chattel, which in this case means the object of the gaze, and becomes a pure eye; her body atrophies, but she *sees*. And she then begins to manipulate Flint, through his desire for her return and for her sex, and even lures him by a series of false letters to look for her in the North. The power she resists is epistemic and linguistic, and so, finally, is the power she constructs for herself out of her virtue and her concealment. (1998: 54)

As with Douglass, the primary aim of Jacobs' narrative is to argue for the inhumanity of the institution of slavery. This necessitates that a reader have sympathy and compassion for her situation. To that end, she aims to facilitate identification between her white female readers and the condition of enslavement. This is revealed in one of the most powerful and complex confessional moments in her text:

> Pity me, and pardon me, O virtuous reader! You never knew what it is to be a slave; to be entirely unprotected by law or custom; to have the laws reduce you to the condition of a chattel, entirely subject to the will of another. You never exhausted your ingenuity in avoiding the snares, and eluding the power of a hated tyrant; you never shuddered at the sound of his footsteps, and trembled within hearing of his voice. I know I did wrong. No one can feel it more sensibly than I do. The painful and humiliating memory will haunt me til my dying day. Still, in looking back, calmly, on the events of my life, I feel that the slave woman ought not to be judged by the same standard as others. ([1861] 2000: 61–2)

In this passage, Jacobs removes the 'shield', however briefly, and makes her reader 'see' as she does. By encouraging empathy, Jacobs attempts to collapse the distance between herself and the white female reader – indeed, she incites readers to consider how white and black women alike suffer as victims of the institution of slavery. A white female reader may well know what it is like to be 'chattel' and to fear a tyrant within the institution of marriage in the nineteenth century, provoking comparison between the roles of slaveholder and husband and condemning the discourse of paternalism used to justify the authority of both. Jacobs' argument, here, is revolutionary in many ways. She insists on common ground, shared experiences between white and black women. She insists on the capacity for empathy and compassion – and, perhaps, alliances (?) – among these women. She argues that 'the slave woman ought not to be judged by the same standard as others', thus opening the shocking possibility (another 'loophole') of alternative value systems, cultural standards, modes of relationship between citizens.

Such an argument might be complicated by the fact that, towards the end of her narrative, Jacobs makes clear her aspirations:

> Reader, my story ends with freedom; not in the usual way, with marriage. I and my children are now free! We are as free from the power of slaveholders as are the white people of the north; and though

> that, according to my ideas, is not saying a great deal, it is a vast improvement in *my* condition. The dream of my life is not yet realized. I do not sit with my children in a home of my own. I still long for a hearthstone of my own, however humble. I wish it for my children's sake far more than for my own. ([1861] 2000: 224–5)

To the extent that Jacobs expresses the desire for property, she continues to make her claim to be included within, and interpellated by, Berlant's (1997) notion of 'abstract personhood' (the sovereign, property owning individual). Jacobs' desire, and its expression, function also to critique a culture in which, as a free woman, she is still not granted the same privileges as white men, and in which her situation at the conclusion of the text does not seem far removed from the situation she outlines in her opening chapter: 'The reader probably knows that no promise or writing given to a slave is legally binding; for, according to Southern laws, a slave, *being* property, can *hold* no property' ([1861] 2000: 8). Being free in the north is 'not saying a great deal' ([1861] 2000: 225), making it clear that slavery and inequality are not problems confined to the South alone. As such, Jacobs' narrative ends ambivalently, reflecting her continuing belief in the 'national promise' of democracy, even as it explicitly reveals her disappointment and anger regarding the fact that the promise is not being kept. There is no sign that it will be kept in the near future (Jacobs' claim that her desires are for her children, rather than herself, suggests that if the promise is kept, it may be future generations who receive its material advantages, not Jacobs herself). That the act of writing and publishing her text is also implicated in this situation is suggested by P. Gabrielle Foreman's claim that Jacobs 'sells her voice in order to secure and express private ownership – not of her body – but of its discursive embodiments, her voice and text themselves' (Foreman, in Garfield and Zafar 1996: 80). Of Equiano's text, Carretta argues:

> Through a combination of natural ability, accident, and determination, Equiano seized every opportunity to rise from the legal status of being an object to be sold by others to become an international celebrity, the story of whose life became his most valuable possession. (Carretta, in Firsch 2007: 57)

Producing autobiography – the property of one's self – helps to confirm the sovereignty of the self, even as it objectifies the self (the self is what is objectified, sold, in the autobiography).

All of the writers in this chapter produce autobiography – a public record of the self – in order to claim private ownership of their bodies and texts. The 'epistemic and linguistic' power, which Sartwell describes as being both resisted and forged by Jacobs, is similarly achieved in the construction of her autobiography. Like all the texts studied in this chapter, Jacobs' autobiography constitutes an act of self-presentation, written for the purposes of making the self known in a certain way. In very different, and often contradictory, ways, though, the autobiographies examined here constitute multiple 'loopholes'. Those loopholes represent the gap or absence generated by an empty (Enlightenment?) promise of democracy. In Riley's terms, they expose the 'productive alienation' caused by the difficulties or impossibility of 'moving towards and accepting some externally given account of a self, which I then take home as mine' (2000: 2). This is another kind of loophole – one created by difficulties encountered in describing oneself as an American or a person. This situation is fascinatingly dramatised by Equiano, Douglass and Jacobs, in particular, who use a genre associated with the development of the Enlightenment subject, in order to show their insistence that they be recognised, and their problems in being recognised, as that subject. Franklin installs himself as a sovereign self, precisely by offering himself as a model for others to be copied; he can afford to objectify himself in this way. The other writers discussed in this chapter cannot do this. In many ways, it is because their identities are not, perhaps, sufficiently their own, that they cannot give them away (in the sense of making explicit acts of self-presentation or offering themselves as models to be imitated). These texts do not necessarily subscribe (only) to Enlightenment values, but are written and published in a world where those values are dominant; they therefore use autobiography to protest the values it supposedly represents. These texts also comprise 'loopholes' in that they represent imaginative spaces, in which alternative futures can be envisaged. They express hope in an America which will keep that national promise, and their autobiographies work to make that America a reality. With the possible exception of Franklin, all of the texts examined here make even more radical claims, suggesting that the sovereign, modern subject of Enlightenment thought is only one of many 'externally given accounts' of self-description (Riley 2000: 2), thus challenging the privileging of white, Western epistemologies. Ultimately, these texts support Leigh Gilmore's claim that 'autobiography provokes fantasies of the real' (1994: 16).

CHAPTER 2

(Un)Representative Selves

My life has been the poem I would have writ;
But I could not both live and utter it.

(Thoreau [1849] 1985: 279)

My autobiography always arrives from somewhere outside me; my narrating *I* is really anybody's, promiscuously. Never mind the coming-of-age story of my life; simply to enunciate that initial 'I' makes me slow down in confusion. (Riley 2000: 58)

The passages above comprise something like a knot of important 'properties' central to autobiography, which can be understood as ultimately pertaining to conundrums of representation. Why, and how, represent one's life in writing? Who, or what, does one represent? This chapter begins by attempting to elucidate those 'properties'.

In *A Week on the Concord and Merrimack Rivers* (1849), Henry David Thoreau, who subsequently authored one of the most important nineteenth century American autobiographical texts – *Walden* (1854) – seemingly confesses a failure to write autobiography. The failure is described as the inability to represent a life: 'I could not both live and utter it'. This apparent confession of failure – and it may not be a confession of failure at all, but something else entirely – forces consideration of a difficult question: that of how writing a life (autobiography) relates to living a life. In implying that living has taken precedence over the act of writing, it is suggested that recording a life may hinder or impede living it. If there is an element of choice in the apparent decision of the 'I' to 'live', rather than 'utter' his life, then writing autobiography is rejected, in favour of engagement with the world – an engagement, it is suggested, which may be more ethically and politically imperative and valuable than the act of writing. The poem that the 'I' 'would have writ' does not exist; so, should we conclude that the speaker has privileged living over utterance? Crucially, the couplet stages the relationship between living a life and writing a life as not simply a question of representation (how to write a life?), but also as a question of ethics. Is it good to write autobiography (as opposed to, say, living a good life)? What good can an autobiography do? Of course, it is also possible to read the couplet as conveying the fact that the speaker has *no* choice: the imperative to live overrides the ability to 'utter'.

The declaration of failure voiced in the couplet usefully highlights the problems of definition and categorisation which attend autobiography here, relating to form and genre, in particular. Why should the speaker's life ('life' as synonym for autobiography or not?) be a *poem*? Does the speaker say that his life is a 'poem' to suggest that the written life is a more ordered, constructed, beautiful version of the life lived – a tidying-up, making more presentable of the awkward, messy business of living? But that raises questions about truth and reference – two perennially vexing issues in relation to autobiography. If autobiography is a representation of the life, in that it is (only) a construction of the life, then perhaps the autobiography is not a truthful rendering of the life. Or, maybe, the speaker suggests that his life has turned out not to be a poem, but it has turned out to be something else.

But, if so, what do we make of the rhyming couplet? The speaker's confession of inability to produce a poem of his life looks suspiciously like a poem (or part of a poem). The first-person pronouns and the confessional tone seem suspiciously like autobiography, while the use of rhyme ensures that the 'I' further accrues to itself the authority of the persona of a lyric poem (of course, the 'I' of the lyric poem need not signal the personal voice of the poet). So is the couplet *not* suggesting that, for this speaker, autobiography is impossible? Could it be suggesting that the only 'true' autobiography is one which confesses its own failure and inadequacy?

The word 'utter' only adds to the perplexities. Does 'utter' refer to both writing ('writ') and speaking? What is the difference between writing and speaking an autobiography? The couplet may not constitute a confession of failure if the speaker is only saying that he cannot 'utter' (speak) his autobiography; his couplet, after all, may be an attempt to *write* it. The couplet's 'I' also refers both to the speaker who has authored, or will author, the life and the individual who has lived the life. This emphasises the interrelatedness of living a life and writing a life (the complexly related 'self', 'life' and 'writing' of autobiography), contradicting the speaker's distinction between the two acts. This interrelatedness challenges the claim of failure articulated in the couplet and, therefore, adds to uncertainty about what this declaration actually constitutes. Is it not autobiography, in the form of a poem? Also, that lyric 'I' serves as a painful reminder of the point Riley makes, above, that the first person pronoun, indicator of individual identity, is not a signifier of uniqueness (this moment of her analysis, too, takes the form of something like a declaration of failure to write autobiography). The pronoun 'I' is 'promiscuous', in that it represents, or belongs to, everyone (so, to no one); it is the property of no individual alone.

Perhaps most difficult of all, the speaker's declaration is complicated by his complex tenses. The couplet's personal pronouns ensure that the temporal location of the speaker and the autobiography are difficult to place. The 'I' occupies an awkward, undefined place between past, present and future and possibly also between reality and fantasy ('My life has been ...', 'I would have writ'). And if the speaker's life *has been* the poem he would have written, then there is no need for autobiography, because the life *is* the autobiography. The complex tenses reflect what Riley (2000) calls 'a strange retrospective and anticipatory modal logic', in which:

> the voice which speaks from strictly no place to announce that 'where I was as something undefined, there instead I shall establish my name', is itself the vexed grammar of self-description. (Riley 2000: 33–4)

The 'I' in this couplet, then, articulates the anxieties that surround articulating an autobiographical 'I'. It shows the difficulty of making an act of self-presentation, in which the self being described is an *autobiographer* (and, in which, the self possibly fails to describe, or represent, him or herself as one).

Itemising interpretative difficulties generated by Thoreau's couplet is not necessarily to resolve them (this discussion, like the couplet, should make a complicated, disingenuous confession of failure at this point). But the purpose of this discussion is not to cite difficulties and then retreat from them. The couplet is useful for the simple fact that, like the promiscuous 'I', the problems it raises are not its speaker's only. They are pertinent to consideration of any autobiography. This chapter examines four important autobiographical texts published in the nineteenth and early twentieth centuries: Thoreau's *Walden* (1854), Walt Whitman's 'Song of Myself' (1855), Henry Adams's *The Education of Henry Adams* (1916) and Gertrude Stein's *The Autobiography of Alice B. Toklas* (1933).

Each negotiates the relationship between living a life and writing a life, even if only to make complex, disingenuous articulations of failure in negotiating that relationship – failure to write autobiography.

It is worth hesitating over the fact that this opening discussion has installed Thoreau's couplet (the questions it raises, the difficulties in answering them) as representative of difficulties present in *all* autobiography. This is in spite of the fact that representativeness is one of the most important, most politically and ethically challenging properties of autobiography. What might be the costs of installing Thoreau's couplet, and then the four titles listed above, as representative of properties of autobiography? It is not clear that the couplet encourages such a 'representative' reading. The speaker refers to nobody else; he does not claim to describe the situation of anyone other than himself. Before offering readings of the four autobiographies, it is important to consider that question of 'representativeness' in some detail.

As Leigh Gilmore notes, and as explored in the previous chapter of this textbook, autobiography can be considered as 'a Western mode of self-production, a discourse that is both a corollary to the Enlightenment and its legacy, and which features a rational and representative "I" at its center' (Gilmore 2001: 2). She explains that 'a gender politics related to truth telling has developed in relation to the legacy of the rational man and the ambiguities within self-representation its related excursions entail' (Gilmore 2001: 21). Discussion of a selection of autobiographical texts in the previous chapter revealed that the gesture of proclaiming the autobiographical self as 'exemplary' or 'representative' (the individual's experiences emblematising that of particular groups to which he or she belongs or identifies with) was vital for male and female, white, African-American and transnational autobiographical subjects in various democratic societies. However, the 'rational and representative "I"', which the history of Western autobiography has privileged, has largely been designated as white and masculine. The capacity of an autobiographer to be representative is dictated by the identity politics, and the politics of identification, of any given historical and cultural moment, together with the cultural capital accruing to particular identities. As Gilmore notes, this 'conflation of the value of the text with the value of the autobiographer' can result in limiting constructions of autobiography, impoverished readings of specific autobiographical texts (Gilmore 1994: 17). To be quite clear: because white male subjects have historically been granted more status, privilege and authority in Western cultures, autobiographies of these subjects are more likely to be considered valuable and truthful, emblematic of the cultures in which they participate and of relevance to others – representative. If this sounds tautological, another confusing hermeneutic knot, that is because it is.

The history of autobiography production and criticism reflects this circular logic. As white, Western, middle-class male subjects were more likely to be considered representative, their autobiographies have more often been attributed canonical status and have been more frequently read, taught and written about. Autobiographies of female and non-white subjects have been less frequently granted canonical status and have received less critical attention and praise (Gilmore 2001: 20–2). While this situation has changed significantly over the last 40 years or so, and will be described in subsequent chapters, these authors' claims to tell the truth, as well as their capacities to be representative, are (still) construed as more complex and contested.

Central to any assessment of the political and ethical aims central to many American autobiographies, then, are questions pertaining to who an autobiographer speaks for, or on behalf of, and the strategies by which they attempt to do so. It is, after all, by contending that his or her life story has some educative value for others that many autobiographers seek to avoid the accusations of self-indulgence and vanity which might attend the act of writing autobiography. And yet, to the extent that an autobiographer claims that his or her text has some relevance to the experiences of others, he or she is claiming to represent those others, whether that claim is made explicitly or not. This risks appropriating or silencing those others' voices and experiences. Gilmore asks the necessary questions with which scholars of autobiography must engage:

> If autobiography helps to install a sovereign subject, what is risked and gained by deposing such sovereignty? How does autobiography's rhetoric of rights and privileges efface its narrowing constraints? Further, how does one lay claim to, or discover, a nonrepresentative self? (2001: 21)

This chapter aims both to acknowledge and unsettle some ideas relating to that property of 'representativeness', by offering readings of a (necessarily selective) group of American autobiographies. To that end, it is worth mentioning Gilmore's fascinating – if often confusing – use of metaphor and metonymy as figures for understanding autobiography – a discussion culminating in her description of 'metonymy as the trope through which autobiography figures the real' (Gilmore 1994: 79). She initially understands metaphor and metonymy as figures for identity in autobiography:

> To prefer one figure to another in a discourse of identity is to repre-sent the place of the self in the world differently: a metonym has meaning in context, as when feminists contend that women autobi-ographers represent the self in relation to others. A metaphor does not depend on a real situation for meaning; rather, it isolates an ideal and draws an analogy between essences, as when the early autobio-graphy scholar Georges Gusdorf claimed that the autobiographical self derives its meaning outside the community and in relation to a higher self. A metaphor has one 'proper' interpretation; a metonym allows for a variety of arrangements and indeed resists the way in which metaphors mean. (1994: 78–9)

There are many problems with this analysis, of which the most serious are the implicit suggestions of essentialist notions of gendered identity and writing and the claims that metaphor does 'not depend on a real situation' and has only one 'proper' meaning (all of which I would dispute, although I do like the fact that the words 'proper' and 'depend' are important to Gilmore's argument here). But Gilmore's identifica-tion of metonymy as particularly important to autobiography has value and will be considered in various ways in the remaining chapters of this textbook. For the purposes of this chapter, it is important to note that metonymy offers a useful way of understanding how representative-ness is achieved and operates. When an individual grants himself (or is granted) the capacity to be exemplary, to represent a particular group, this can be likened to metonymy, in that a part (the individual) is made to represent the whole (the group he represents). As discussed, that metonymic move, which James M. Cox calls a 'synechdochic strategy' (Cox 1971: 270), is undertaken for political and ethical purposes, but often has dubious consequences (the manner in which Franklin displaces or excludes certain identities in the act of declaring himself a model 'fit to be imitated' is an obvious example). It is also worth noting a further paradox of representativeness, which may be especially pertinent for American autobiography. Many of the subjects occupying canonical status in histories of American autobiography are, nonetheless, outsider figures, who variously emphasise how they are 'unrepresentative'. Yet, it is precisely that status which has rendered them, in American culture, particularly capable of being representative. Gilmore's claim that autobiography offers the opportunity for 'representing the self as utterly unique and, on precisely this basis, able to stand for others' (Gilmore 2001: 19) is clearly relevant here. That metonymic move, integral to the process of installing oneself as representative, also functions to *place* or locate an individual in relation to his or her culture, although how to describe this relationship and location is difficult. It *might* be understood as a process of bringing an individual from outside to inside (from periphery to centre).

On 4 July 1845, Thoreau embarked upon an important 'experiment' (78). He withdrew from his local community in Concord, Massachusetts, and took up residence on a small area of land rented by Emerson, near Walden Pond. His action reveals a belief in (and privileging of) the capacities of the natural world to provide opportunities for self-examination. It also reveals a conviction that self-examination generates valuable truths about the self and its relation to its environment. His action suggests that the individual and his or her acts of interpretation should be privileged over laws and social conventions, which should not be obeyed unthinkingly. As such, Thoreau's attitudes are broadly representative of the influential philosophy of Transcendentalism, particularly influential in American culture from the 1830s to the 1850s (Myerson 2000: xxv–xxxvii). In addition, it should be clear that autobiographical writing might have special importance as a vehicle for communicating the Transcendalists' valorisation of individuality and self-expression and emphasis on the pursuit of truths via self-examination. However, like the 'I' in his couplet, the philosophical and political position together with the ethical stance of Thoreau's 'experiment' (a term which could usefully describe both the life and the writing of the life), are difficult to locate. Three details suffice to illustrate this. Firstly, Thoreau structures his narrative according to the cycle of a single year – 'for convenience, putting the experience of two years into one' (78) – which signals a decision to dispense with literal fact, in favour of a more symbolic truth, and has, for some critics, compromised the text's status as autobiography (Varner Gunn 1977). Certainly, it is a gesture which shows that Thoreau may prioritise the writing of a life over the living of it. He is focused on the values and lessons he wishes his experience to communicate, rather than on scrupulously recounting those experiences. Secondly, while Thoreau claims that his experiment began on this date 'by accident' (78), he notes the date. Whether Thoreau's two-year withdrawal from society constitutes a retreat from politics and a rejection of society (an attempt to place himself 'outside') or a political act, indicative of active partici-pation in his culture (he remains 'inside'), is unclear. His experiment is a political assertion of individual independence, registering discon-tent. But at the same time, Thoreau locates himself within a national mythology, underscoring his status as an archetypal American – repre-sentative of his culture, even as he lives at a remove from it. Thirdly, the circumstances surrounding Thoreau's removal are ambiguous, as he relates them:

> Near the end of March, 1845, I borrowed an axe and went down to the woods by Walden Pond, nearest to where I intended to build my house, and began to cut down some tall arrowy white pines, still in their youth, for timber. It is difficult to begin without borrowing, but perhaps it is the most generous course thus to permit your fellow-men to have an interest in your enterprise. (38)

Thoreau's emphasis on generosity, prompted by his discussion of borrowing, signals that his central concern is about relationships; how or whether the individual can live well with others. Acknowledging depen-dence on the generosity of others undermines the narrative of individu-alism and independence often foregrounded and celebrated in the text. After all, Thoreau's status as a 'representative man' rests on the fact that many readers read *Walden* as charting a narrative of self-discovery and self-construction, in which the individual is linked to national history, as in Franklin's and Douglass' autobiographies. Like them, Thoreau consciously offers himself as an exemplar, providing a model of living for others, even if he both seriously and playfully resists this status: '[The reader] will not venture to put my abstemiousness to the test unless he has a well-stocked larder' (56); 'I would not have anyone adopt *my* mode of living on any account' (64–5). Like Franklin and Douglass, too, Thoreau is fond of parables. He frequently enlists a didactic tone – 'We need to be provoked, – goaded like oxen, as we are, into a trot' (99) – and tends to offer life lessons in the form of maxims – 'The mass of men lead lives of quiet desperation' (9); 'Instead of noblemen, let us have noble villages of men' (101). Arguably, though, Thoreau is more explicit than either Franklin or Douglass in noting the reliance on others necessary to implement his project. He borrows an axe, he lives on land rented by Emerson. Thoreau converts what might be considered an unenviable condition of dependence on others' generosity into a generous act, one which, moreover, allows 'fellow-men' an 'interest' in his enterprise. The word 'interest' should call to mind the discussion of Equiano's text in the previous chapter. It is in engaging the reader's interest, representing the 'interests' of certain groups, that both Thoreau and Equiano's autobiographies, like many others, find their ethical impetus (and justification for the autobiographer's role as 'representative').

However, the nature of the 'interest' readers may share in Thoreau's enterprise is unclear. Thoreau's comment above, dissuading others from adopting his mode of living, is prefaced by an anecdote about a young man who claims he would follow Thoreau's example *'if he had the means'* (64, emphasis in original). Thoreau's 'experiment' is enabled by his friends' resources – land, tools – and by relationships and assets, in turn afforded by his own social capital – his class and gender entail that he can acquire education, leisure time – not all of which (or any of which) would have been available to many of his readers. Thoreau's reference to 'fellow-men' is quite specific. On many occasions, Thoreau shows awareness of the situation of the poor and disenfranchised: 'Some of you, we all know, are poor, find it hard to live, are sometimes, as it were, gasping for breath' (8). However, his 'we' refers both to 'all' and to a more specific group; the majority of readers as opposed to 'some', the 'you', pointing to a larger uncertainty about just who Thoreau is speaking to, on behalf of. Arguing that *Walden* makes use of generic conventions of the travel book, which was popular in the nineteenth century, Richard J. Schneider suggests that Thoreau can be understood as a 'tour guide' and that the reader 'finds himself or herself in the situation of a tourist signing on to tour a strange land, only to find the tour guide heading toward the tourist's own home' (Schneider, in Myerson 1995: 93, 94). However, while 'tour guide' sounds friendly and helpful, Thoreau's attitude towards individuals he encounters in the text, like his attitude to readers, can often be condescending, unsympathetic, if not actually obstructive and hostile (consider, for example, the discussion of John Field in the 'Baker Farm' chapter). 'Economy', the opening chapter of *Walden*, takes the form of a critique of aspects of American culture, which Thoreau believes to constitute impediments in the way of an individual's self-development, virtue and happiness. He attacks frivolity and luxury and, along with many Transcendentalist thinkers and writers, is ambivalent about many of the developments and changes taking place in the increasingly urbanised, commercialised America of the mid-nineteenth century. His advocacy of engagement with the natural world could be read as a rejection of the present, illustrative of a desire – problematic, because possibly naïve, romanticised – to return to an agrarian past. Thoreau does not directly accuse readers of complicity in creating the cultural conditions he detests, but this is implied. Similarly, his privileging of the act of reading and reading well – 'The works of the great poets have never yet been read by mankind, for only great poets can read them' (95) – may mean that he addresses himself to an elite few who meet his high standards, who share his views (or he addresses himself to no one, since it appears that nobody has yet met his standards). Ultimately, *Walden* suggests that those most able to adopt Thoreau's mode of living, either literally or in terms of appreciating the lessons he has to offer, are those who are most like him and who are, therefore, primarily addressed by the text.

That gesture of 'borrowing', of converting the potentially disempowering position of dependence into one of virtuous representativeness, usefully illuminates Thoreau's complex relationship to the Franklinian American autobiographical tradition. Thoreau deliberately invokes that tradition for the purposes of locating himself within it. In a (by now familiar) tautological move, it is precisely *because* he places himself within that tradition that Thoreau can claim the status of 'representative man'. But to locate Thoreau solely, or comfortably, within this tradition is to tell only a partial story. Thoreau also invokes that tradition in order to grant himself the latitude necessary to distance himself from it. This is one means by which he engages in the practice of reform which Myerson identifies as central to the social project of Transcendentalism (2000: xxxiv). The dangers of failing to recognise this are evident in Markus Poetzsch's observation that *Walden* is 'a direct endorsement of the self-authored life' – a claim prompted by a desire to read Thoreau as a Franklinian figure (2008: 5). Poetzsch cites a passage from *Walden* as evidence of such 'endorsement':

> Moreover, I, on my side, require of every writer, first or last, a simple and sincere account of his own life, and not merely what he has heard of other men's lives; some such account as he would send to his kindred from a distant land; for if he has lived sincerely, it must have been in a different land to me. (2008: 5–6)

Despite Poetzsch's claim, Thoreau positions himself here as a *reader*, in addition to author; the passage is taken from the opening of *Walden*, in which Thoreau attempts to outline what readers should expect from his text, by describing what he, as a reader, ideally expects from a writer. In so doing, he illustrates Nancy Miller's 'two propositions' about the purposes of autobiography:

> the first, that the subjects of life writing (memoir, diary, essay, confession) are as much others as ourselves; the second, that reading the lives of other people with whom we do *not* identify has as much to tell us (if not more) about our lives as the lives with which we do. On the assumption that we read autobiographical writing in order to learn something about ourselves as well as about others, disidentification takes us as readers on a (sometimes circuitous, which is the whole point) journey back to ourselves. (Miller 2002: xv–xvi)

By putting himself in the role of the reader, Thoreau attempts to make himself 'other'. On occasion, in *Walden*, he explicitly urges readers *not* to see him as a Franklinian model 'fit to be imitated', as this would emphasise the similarities between Thoreau and his readers. The aim of his text appears to be to encourage readers to embark on the 'sometimes circuitous' journey of self-discovery which Miller outlines (think, also, of Gilmore's 'related excursions' of self-representation). But this, too, is only a partial reading: Thoreau does not reject the Franklinian model. He only encourages his readers to see him as 'other', to the extent that they will, ultimately, in acknowledging shared 'otherness' with Thoreau, read him as representative. Poetzsch (2008) analyses the passage, which he understands as a 'direct endorsement of the self-authored life', as follows:

> By questioning whether anyone has lived sincerely, [Thoreau] casts doubt on the possibility that anyone, at least in industrialised America, has written a sincere autobiography. The necessary precondition for autobiographical sincerity is not an act of earnest soul-searching or, still less, an assertion of literary talent; nothing more and nothing less than the living of a simple and sincere life will do. Autobiographical products (and theories, one might add) presuppose an autobiographical praxis. (2008: 391)

Poetzsch's claim that Thoreau advocates self-authorship leads him to conclude that Thoreau does not recognise the possibility of 'sincere autobiography'. This attributes dubious motives or moral shortcomings to other autobiographers and implies that autobiography is impossible. But it is only by invoking an autobiographical tradition that Poetzsch understands Thoreau as a representative American man. And, yes, Thoreau is trying to negotiate the relationship between autobiographical theory and praxis (living and writing a life), but not by disparaging an entire autobiographical tradition. Instead, Thoreau attempts to set out an ethics for reading and writing autobiography, which *also* offers a model for living a good life – one in which writing the life improves the quality of the life lived and which 'permit [s] [his] fellow-men to have an interest in [his] enterprise'. Theory and praxis are linked here, because that model depends upon the interrelationship – interchangeability, even – of the roles of reader and writer. Poetzsch misreads the text, because of his limited and inflexible understanding of what an autobiography should look like and do.

This misreading is additionally illustrated by another claim Poetzsch makes – that Walden Pond, an admittedly central symbol in the text, functions as an analogy for autobiography. By 'autobiography', Poetzsch appears to refer to both the text of *Walden* and the genre more widely. Poetzsch examines the pond's symbolic properties. He argues that it represents the mysteriousness of the local – its hidden depths are a reflection of the difficulties of interpretation that the text poses for the reader. He concludes his article by arguing that:

> Walden like *Walden* is the text of a life, yet its subject is not Thoreau alone. The pond, rather, is an autobiographical template upon which anyone may cast his/her image. Its permanence, depth, unsullied purity, and sensitivity to the slightest movement upon its surface enable the reflection of any life, any subject. There are preconditions of course, the most important being a willingness to leave the clutter of the world and come to Walden's shores, to strip away the masks and postures of life and push out, denuded, upon its waters [...] (2008: 399)

This analysis can stand as representative of the problems which arise in reading a text by a 'representative man', in a manner which attends insufficiently to the particularities and limits of that representative capacity. The pond is *not* an 'autobiographical template' for any life, any subject; far from it, as the discussion of the limited readership Thoreau may have in mind suggests. The limited readership 'preconditions' the text. If Walden Pond truly is an analogy for *Walden* the text, the subject and life it reflects is Thoreau's. It is very much of a specific time and place. Fascinatingly, Poetzsch's criticism responds to its own simplistic reading of Thoreau's text, as communicating a Franklinian message along the lines of 'learn from me; copy me', revealed by his envisaging of the reader (any reader) pushing out across the pond to repeat Thoreau's 'experiment'. As an alternative to this reading, it is worth noting Michael R. Fischer's claim that Thoreau leaves Walden, 'as if to discourage us from copying his experiment or taking it too literally' (Fischer, in Fayre 1992: 103).

A more productive means of thinking about the contradictions and limitations of Thoreau's text is found by considering Thoreau's relationship to the loon, which Schneider calls an 'ambiguous and troubling symbol' (Schneider, in Myerson 1995: 101), as an analogy for the relationship between Thoreau and the reader:

As I was paddling along the north shore one very calm October afternoon, for such days especially they settle on to the lakes, like the milkweed down, having looked in vain over the pond for a loon, suddenly one, sailing out from the shore toward the middle a few rods in front of me, set up his wild laugh and betrayed himself. I pursued with a paddle and he dived, but when he came up I was nearer than before. He dived again, but I miscalculated the direction he would take, and we were fifty rods apart when he came to the surface this time, for I had helped to widen the interval; and again he laughed long and loud, and with more reason than before. He manoeuvred so cunningly that I could not get within half a dozen rods of him. Each time, when he came to the surface, turning his head this way and that, he coolly surveyed the water and the land, and apparently chose his course so that he might come up where there was the widest expanse of water and at the greatest distance from the boat. It was surprising how quickly he made up his mind and put his resolve into execution. He led me at once to the widest part of the pond, and could not be driven from it. While he was thinking one thing in his brain, I was endeavouring to divine his thought in mine. It was a pretty game, played on the smooth surface of the pond, a man against a loon. Suddenly your adversary's checker disappears beneath the board, and the problem is to place yours nearest to where his will appear again. Sometimes he would come up unexpectedly on the opposite side of me, having apparently passed directly under the boat. So long-winded was he and so unweariable, that when he had swum farthest he would immediately plunge again, nevertheless; and then no wit could divine where in the deep pond, beneath the smooth surface, he might be speeding his way like a fish, for he had time and ability to visit the bottom of

the pond in its deepest part. [...] Once or twice I saw a ripple where
he approached the surface, just put his head out to reconnoitre, and
instantly dived again. I found that it was as well for me to rest on my
oars and wait his reappearing as to endeavour to calculate where he
would rise; for again and again, when I was straining my eyes over the
surface one way, I would suddenly be startled by his unearthly laugh
behind me. But why, after displaying so much cunning, did he invari-
ably betray himself the moment he came up by that loud laugh? Did
not his white breast betray him? He was indeed a silly loon, I thought.
[...] I concluded that he laughed in derision of my efforts, confident of
his own resources. (210–11)

Understanding Thoreau's relationship with the loon as providing a
model for his relationship with the reader, depends upon participation
in the acts of reading and interpretation dramatised in this passage –
acts which reflect the influence of the Puritan theological practice of
typology on Transcendentalist thought. By transforming the loon into
a symbol, Thoreau finds, in nature, the source of literal truths, but
his acts of perception and interpretation also provide more abstract,
symbolic truths. The 'pretty game' of searching for the loon vividly
dramatises the complex processes of reading and interpretation in which
Thoreau is engaged; acts of identification and dis-identification mark the
relations between Thoreau and the loon and between Thoreau and his
ideal readers. These readers, it should be reiterated, are reflections of
Thoreau, in that they are generally imagined as belonging to his gender,
race and class, but from whom, nonetheless, he 'others' himself, as a
crucial part of sending the reader on a 'related excursion', intended to
culminate in the reader finally installing Thoreau as representative. This
shifting ground of identification and dis-identification is achieved by
Thoreau's use of the word 'your', which describes himself, but which
simultaneously functions as a means of allowing the reader an 'interest'
in the game (it encourages readers to engage in such searches of their
own). The use of 'your' also posits reference in the text as unlocatable
(who is the text addressing? Everyone? A select group only? Thoreau
alone? Nobody?). Schneider describes the loon as a 'friendly but teasing
adversary' (103). It is hard to determine who is winning the game –
Thoreau is unsure whether to read the loon's laugh as a sign of unreason,
which betrays the loon's location, or, rather, as a mockery of his own
attempts to determine where the loon will appear next.

The game of searching for the loon might also be understood as the pursuit of identity itself. Riley argues:

> So often conceived as a thing to be unearthed, my identity (if I am forced to locate such an object at all) may turn out to be not so much a matter of what it is, but of where it is [...]. (2000: 9)

This understanding of the importance of the *location* of identity leads Riley to consider 'some idea of an identity which is founded largely in dispersal' (2000: 9). Such a notion of identity sheds further light on the gesture of offering the self as gift – a model for others – often present in American autobiographies (giving the self as gift is also to disperse the self). It shows why that metonymic move of installing the self as representative is self-interested, ethically ambivalent and highly risky: 'Giving myself away in order to find myself, I might even feel perversely and mysteriously generous [...] There is another version of giving myself away, which results in losing myself' (54). The ambiguity of Thoreau's gesture of giving the self away is revealed in Ira Brooker's observation that 'by extolling the virtues of the Walden experiment in print, [Thoreau] gave the public access to his formula' (2004: 150). If Thoreau's text encourages others to go to Walden, as he has done, this risks destroying the qualities which make Walden special in the first place: it is largely uninhabited. It may turn Walden into a tourist destination, thus bringing capitalist enterprise to Walden (it may have been largely protected from this enterprise so far). It may, therefore, encourage readers to participate in colonial or imperialist logic and enterprise (visiting Walden becomes about knowing or mastering the natural world).

A notion of identity as dispersal, though, enables the text to be read outside any narrow or exceptionalist context. Thoreau's many allusions to non-Western and ancient texts not only identify him as a Transcendalist, for whom the reading of texts and learning from the past are central, but also support an understanding of him as a transnational figure, who, despite his focus on the local and specific, is nonetheless very aware of the larger world he inhabits. Paul Giles reads *Walden* as confirming his claim that:

> one consequence of a transnational approach to American literature is to disturb any idea of it as a homogenous or inclusive cultural field. The crucial point is precisely not to make United States perspectives synonymous with those of the wider world. (Giles 2003: 72)

But lest this be too generous a reading of Thoreau's autobiographical project, it might be useful to return to a passage near the beginning of *Walden*, thus making the 'circuitous journey', which Miller suggests that reading autobiography may necessitate:

> In any weather, at any hour of the day or night, I have been anxious to improve the nick of time, and notch it on my stick too; to stand on the meeting of two eternities, the past and future, which is precisely the present moment; to toe that line. You will pardon some obscurities, for there are more secrets in my trade than in most men's, and yet not voluntarily kept, but inseparable from its very nature. I would gladly tell all that I know about it, and never paint 'No Admittance' on my gate. (17)

Thoreau's focus on relationships and neighbourliness does not mean that he does not desire an identity clearly marked as his own. He warns the reader, here, that he will not tell everything he knows; though he says this is not a voluntary withholding of information, he is not keen to give himself away completely. This gesture of refusal – refusal of disclosure, refusal to surrender bounds between self and other – means that Thoreau insists on retaining the privacy of the property owning sovereign self (he would 'never paint "No Admittance" on [his] gate'), thus preserving all of the confusions in the couplet with which this chapter opened.

Walt Whitman's 'Song of Myself', contained in his poetry collection *Leaves of Grass* (1855), is also an 'experiment' in relating the acts of living and writing the life of 'Walt Whitman, a kosmos, of Manhattan the son, / Turbulent, fleshly, sensual, eating, drinking and breeding, / No sentimentalist, no stander above men and women or apart from them, / No more modest than immodest' ([1855] 2009: stanza 24). Like *Walden*, the poem offers a commentary on, and critique of, the vast changes taking place in American culture in the mid-nineteenth century. The poem is notable for the inclusive, expansionist (one might say 'promiscuous') vision of its poetic 'I'; so much so that Brian Harding claims that the text might be understood as aspiring to the status of a 'universal' autobiography (Harding, in Lee 1988: 63). By claiming identification with all Americans, the life written in this text is shared by all. As the text explores what identity and autobiography might mean, it disturbs conventional notions of poetic form and the role of the poet, and, indeed, Betsey Erkkila claims that the poem 'tests the democratic theory of America' (Erkkila, in Cummings 1990: 57).

M. Jimmie Killingsworth argues that:

Whitman represents the people of America in at least three senses. As a writer represents a topic, he reproduces the nation in art. As an elevated official represents a constituency in a republic, he speaks for the nation in the voice of an individual citizen. And as a hero represents the aspirations of the populace as a whole, he models the fullest experience of selfhood. (Killingsworth 2007: 28)

As described here, the three senses of representativeness that Killingsworth cites are thoroughly pedestrian and do not give an indication of the revolutionary nature of Whitman's text. The artist, as a figure who can depict his nation in art, and the writer, as representative 'hero', 'model' of the 'fullest experience of selfhood'; these are well-established ways of conceiving of the role of art and the artist and the possibilities of the autobiographical project, as illustrated in this volume by the discussions of Franklin, Douglass and Thoreau. No less than *Walden*, though, 'Song of Myself' tests the possibilities and limits of both autobiography and a particular model of selfhood. In Whitman's case, the autobiographical 'I' is given the task of – and is presumed capable of – cataloguing, documenting and celebrating American life. As the above self-description suggests, the poem's autobiographical 'I' is portrayed as outcast and rebel. The 'I' frankly acknowledges and explores non-normative sexualities. Traditional value systems are overturned (for example, bodily experience is foregrounded). There is a refusal to perpetuate the hierarchies and inequalities of American culture: 'Why should I pray? Why should I venerate and be ceremonious?' ([1855] 2009: stanza 20). Killingsworth's staid tripartite formula for the modes of representativeness in the poem is, therefore, somewhat misleading. His example of the 'elevated official', in particular, connotes a degree of public authority, which the poem's 'I' does not simply assume, but, rather, has to forge and claim for itself. Often the 'I' does not desire the elected official's respectability; this is precisely where some of the poem's revolutionary quality is to be found. Nonetheless, Killingworth's analysis is useful. Its tripartite formula of representation dramatises tensions between part and whole, and both describes and depends upon strategies of fragmentation and itemisation present in the poem itself. 'Song of Myself' is an autobiography which attempts a kind of 'naming of parts' of America. To achieve this task, the poem's 'I' splits himself into parts, reflecting Riley's notion of identity as dispersal – that risky and ambivalent (metonymic) gesture of giving the self away. The 'I' fragments, in an attempt to itemise and capture the experience of others, to claim identification with all. This is, of course, also an attempt to itemise and capture Whitman himself.

'Song of Myself' is revolutionary (superficially, at least) in claiming equality with all. The 'I' insists that all individuals – women, African-Americans, the poor, the elderly – are equally representative of, and participant in, American national life. The simple fact of cataloguing and including these groups within the poem is designed to recognise them and confer equality. But the 'I' does more than this, claiming intimate knowledge of 'other' experiences, demonstrated in the many acts of imaginative identification performed throughout the poem. Stanza 11 is a particularly useful example. It depicts a 'lady', described as 'all so lonesome', who watches 'twenty-eight young men bathe by the shore'. She is undetected by the young men, but her act is documented by the autobiographical 'I', who not only echoes her act of voyeurism, by watching over the entire scene in omniscient fashion, but presumes to understand her desires and her reactions to the bathers: 'Which of the young men does she like the best? Ah, the homeliest of them is beautiful to her'. In this stanza, the male autobiographical 'I' inhabits the consciousness of an 'other' identity (female, heterosexual). He expresses curiosity about the observing woman's desires ('Where are you off to, lady?') and attempts to record them with sympathy and care. Intriguingly, the 'I' acknowledges its own presence and participation in the scene: 'An unseen hand also pass'd over their bodies, / It descended tremblingly from their temples and ribs'. The autobiographical 'I' is represented by a body part – the hand – which metonymically stands in for Whitman, the writer who records and participates in the scene (the hand writes), in a way inflected by his own desires (the hand caresses the young men). Additionally, it must be asked whether this stanza records events in any 'truthful' sense, as the woman is 'hidden', the hand does not literally caress and so the 'truth', here, may be symbolic, not literal. The stanza reflects on the young men's lack of awareness about the scene in which they participate, noting that 'they do not ask who seizes fast to them' and concluding: 'They do not know who puffs and declines with pendant and bending arch, / They do not think whom they souse with spray'. This stanza, therefore, forces the questions about how an individual life is lived in relation to others, which also mark *Walden*. The ignorance of the young men may be innocent (they don't realise how they affect others), but it might be the ignorance of indifference or selfishness (they don't care about others, only themselves). The role of the 'I' in this stanza is also compromised. Whitman's imaginative identification with the watching woman is predicated on the fact that both she and he observe the bathing men with shared (erotic) interest. Whitman's assumption that the woman assesses the attractiveness of the young men may suggest that Whitman only represents individuals by attributing his own desires and values to them. He also sees the woman only in the abstract, representative of her sex in general ('lady'), defining her in terms of her sexuality (however, the fact that he grants sexual desire to her without censure may be daring and generous). Overall, the 'I' may share the self-centredness and indifference of the young men.

The use of the hand to represent Whitman is also problematic. The hand is detached from the rest of the autobiographer's body, indicative of the writer's reluctance to make himself available for scrutiny (we only see a part of him). This is further supported by the fact that the caressing hand is referred to as 'it', signalling unwillingness to identify openly with the sexual desires the scene illustrates. The disembodied hand might suggest that the autobiographer's identity is fragmented, incomplete, partial (the hand could be anyone's; nothing indicates definitively that it is Whitman's). This acknowledges that some degree of loss of personal identity is one consequence of installing the self as representative, as Franklin does. Yet, if the various ways of reading the hand so far suggest the autobiographer's effacement, the hand obviously signals that Whitman literally has a hand in the scene. He records it – he imagines what the woman and the bathing men are thinking and feeling; most crucially, in possibly limited ways which may reinforce both Whitman's interests and the dominant values of his culture (although these are not always identical). The hand, therefore, illustrates that the autobiographer's representation of the scene is partial, in more ways than one. This risks making the poem's radical claims of equality and inclusion merely superficial.

It is productive to consider Whitman's strategy of imaginative identification with that of Harriet Jacobs, whose slave narrative was discussed in the first chapter of this textbook. Speaking within a cultural context in which she has less authority than her (mostly white) readers, Jacobs' attempts to convince those readers of the inequalities of her society, by encouraging them to imagine what her experience is like ('Pity me, and pardon me, O virtuous reader! You never knew what it is to be a slave; to be entirely unprotected by law or custom' ([1861] 2000: 61)).

This incitement to imaginative empathy is designed to break down the experiential distance caused by difference, by forging ties of identification and sympathy and shared ethical and political aims. Whitman does not do this. Instead, he imagines the experiences of others, inhabiting their identities. Killingsworth notes that the poem 'radically extends the sympathetic imagination associated with eighteenth century poetics and English Romantic poets, the tendency of which is to identify with others to the point of empathetic self-transformation' (2007: 28). These acts of imaginative identification, while motivated by a politics and ethics of inclusion, achieved via sympathy – 'I will not have a single person slighted or left away' (19) – risk colonising, rather than acknowledging, the experiences of others. It seems that often, rather than representing difference, Whitman's notion of identity as dispersal functions to invest others with parts of himself – 'I know perfectly well my own egotism' (42). Kerry Larson notes that the poem's 'I' 'is a site of identification that epitomises the operations of a distinctively democratic empathy', but, ultimately, concludes that 'Whitman's poetics of sympathy is, in short, formal, abstract and mechanical' (Larson, in Cummings 2009: 478, 479) – a reading with which it is difficult to disagree. The impression that the 'I' is engaged in an exercise – at best well-intentioned, but superficial; at worst, insidiously appropriative and coercive – may be experienced by readers, too, who are variously incorporated and excluded by the poem's 'you' – the addressee of the text, who is, by turns, both generic and specific. John B. Mason notes that despite the purportedly dialogic framework of the poem, which invites the voices of others, the text is both 'oratorical and conversational' and that if students feel the oratorical tone to be overwhelming, then they may be 'likely to miss much of the poem's conversation and fail to take their part'. More than this, Mason notes that the poem is 'untypical of a conversation and students *may not want* to take their part' (Mason, in Cummings 1990: 42, my emphasis).

Rather than recognising difference, then, there is a danger that, in 'Song of Myself', differences are flattened out, incorporated into the totality of the poem's 'I': 'Whoever degrades another degrades me, / And whatever is done or said returns at last to me' (24). Additionally, that authoritative, all-encompassing 'I' threatens to undo the text's radical intent, by rendering itself impersonal, anonymous; reading this poem, suspicions may arise that the representative capacities of the 'I' rest on shaky ground or are groundless. The problem with attempts to be

universally representative is that they risk collapse, becoming representative of nothing. That the 'I' is aware of these difficulties does not mean
that they are resolved:

> These are really the thoughts of all men in all ages and lands, they
>   are not original with me,
> If they are not yours as much as mine they are nothing, or next
>   to nothing,
> If they are not the riddle and the untying of the riddle they are
>   nothing,
> If they are not just as close as they are distant they are nothing.
>
> This is the grass that grows wherever the land is and the water is,
> This is the common air that bathes the globe.
>
>   ([1855] 2009: stanza 17)

Sometimes the 'I' clearly strives to represent a totality of experience,
while preserving particularity and difference: 'They are but parts, any
thing is but a part' ([1855] 2009: stanza 45). Despite this, it is Whitman's
'part' which is granted particular authority: 'My knowledge my live
parts, it keeping tally with the meaning of / all things' ([1855] 2009:
stanza 25). Often the 'I' deals with this situation by embracing paradox
both seriously and playfully – 'Do I contradict myself? / Very well
then I contradict myself, / (I am large, I contain multitudes)' ([1855]
2009: stanza 51). This can seem flippant, as if the 'I' is disinclined to
untangle the knot of contradictions presented by 'Song of Myself'.
The poem's conclusion is similarly ambiguous, effectively handing the
task of interpreting and unravelling over to the reader: 'If you want
me again look for me under your boot-soles'; 'Failing to fetch me at
first keep encouraged, / Missing me one place search another, / I stop
somewhere waiting for you' ([1855] 2009: stanza 52). Whitman sounds
like Thoreau's loon, playing a 'pretty game' of hide and seek with the
reader. This final gesture of granting the task of interpretation could be
a generous one, allowing the reader to have an 'interest' in the enterprise
of recording and interpreting Whitman and America. But it might be
read as an abdication of responsibility (Whitman gives up attempting to
resolve contradictions), one that is self-centred, at that. The reader's task
is, quite specifically, all about Whitman; it is suggested that by searching
for him, finding out who he is, America, or even the world, can be read
(Whitman, too, then, can be read as a transnational subject, although he

perhaps does fall into the trap of making America representative of the world).

It is hard not to feel that in 'Song of Myself' the 'I' becomes caught up in its own exuberance and self-celebration to the extent that it overreaches, claiming an America of equals which does not exist in fact. That is, *saying* that all are equal does not make it true (just as, perhaps, saying something is autobiography does not make it so). To put this in the terms of Thoreau's couplet, the speaker's utterance may be more concerned with how he wants life to be lived, than how it is actually being lived. His desire to 'utter' that ideal life expresses that ideal as if it were being lived already. A generous reading of the text might claim that it is precisely in the act of uttering the poem and the life that the poem tries to create the America it so desires, making this autobiography aspire to the qualities of what Eve Sedgwick calls an '*explicit performative utterance*'. This is a kind of utterance in which, as J. L. Austin notes, 'it seems that to utter the sentence (in, of course, the appropriate circumstances) is not to describe my doing [a thing] ... or to state that I am doing it: it is to do it' (Austin 1970, in Sedgwick 2003: 4).

Great-grandson of President and Founding Father John Adams, grandson of American President John Quincy Adams, Henry Adams would clearly seem a candidate for the role of 'representative man'. However, Adams' autobiography, *The Education of Henry Adams* (1916), functions to provide an exploration and explanation of the factors which, it is suggested, make it difficult for Adams to attain that status. Fully aware that the conditions of American modernism render the condition of representativeness thoroughly problematic, Adams portrays himself both sincerely and ironically as a failure; indeed, Andrew West claims that one of the central themes of the autobiography is 'the failure of ducation' (2008: 91). One of Adams' repeated, ironic, mocking refrains is that he believes that he is born in the wrong time: 'What could become of such a child of the seventeenth and eighteenth centuries, when he should wake up to find himself required to play the game of the twentieth?' ([1916] 2008: 9). Discussing the value of Adams' autobiography, Paul A. Bové argues:

> Endlessly, he shows the collapse of Western systems, the inadequacy of inherited institutions, the dangerous persistence of recognisable thoughts, the human errors that result from all these, and the seeming impossibility of the intellect, armed with all the resources American education can provide, to imagine alternatives that will do what is needful. (1996: 100)

Two identities are particularly important to Adams' self-construction, which is put to the purpose of describing and representing the perplexities Bové notes above. He describes himself as a perpetual 'student' – an individual in need of education, someone struggling to find a model by which to live. He also portrays himself as a 'historian' – one who seeks 'a study of relation' ([1916] 2008: 8), that is, a theory which will enable him to make sense of the world in which he lives. The central irony in this ironic text is that it is in Adams' sense of loss and disorientation, in his continued 'failures' of education, in his inability to find a theory which satisfies him, that Adams can be representative. As Matthew A. Taylor argues:

> Pressuring the Emersonian notion of representative men (and the larger American ethos of individualistic self-determination) to the point of implosion, Adams's text makes an example of Adams, representing through his compelled life the impersonal forces compelling our own. (2009: 385)

Adams takes up the question of representation early in his text:

> American literature offers scarcely one working model for high education. The student must go back, beyond Jean Jacques, to Benjamin Franklin, to find a model even of self-teaching. Except in the abandoned sphere of the dead languages, no one has discussed what part of education has, in his personal experience, turned out to be useful, and what not. This volume attempts to discuss it.
>
> As educator, Jean Jacques was, in one respect, easily first; he erected a monument of warning against the Ego. Since his time, and largely thanks to him, the Ego has steadily tended to efface itself, and, for purposes of model, to become a manikin on which the toilet of education is to be draped in order to show the fit or misfit of the clothes. The object of study is the garment, not the figure. The tailor adapts the manikin as well as the clothes to his patron's wants. The tailor's object, in this volume, is to fit young men, in universities or elsewhere, to be men of the world, equipped for any emergency; and the garment offered to them is meant to show the faults of the patchwork fitted on their fathers.
>
> At the utmost, the active-minded young man should ask of his teacher only mastery of his tools. The young man himself, the subject of education, is a certain form of energy; the object to be gained is economy of his force; the training is partly the clearing away of

obstacles, partly the direct application of effort. Once acquired, the tools and models may be thrown away.

The manikin, therefore, has the same value as any other geometrical figure of three or more dimensions, which is used for the study of relation. For that purpose it cannot be spared; it is the only measure of motion, of proportion, of human condition; it must have the air of reality; must be taken for real; must be taken as if it had life. Who knows! Possibly it had! ([1916] 2008: 7–8)

Adams is ambivalent about locating himself within the tradition of American autobiography, of which he cites Franklin as representative. His allusion to Franklin is not made in a whole-hearted spirit of allegiance to the aims of Franklin's autobiography or the kind of identity constructed within it. It is, rather, Rousseau, and his warnings *against* ego, which receive Adams' attention. Adams' stress on the importance of education suggests that he subscribes to the notion of autobiography as didactic, but he appears reluctant to embrace Franklin's model of using the self as a didactic tool, something which also amounts to self-promotion (hence, Adams' interest in Rousseau). Adams' focus is, then, not on his (own) autobiographical self, but more generally on the influence of cultural forces on the development of the individual: 'The object of study is the garment, not the figure'. Nonetheless, Adams cannot do without a model of selfhood in the text; the object of study may be the garment, but the aim is to study the relation of the garment to the figure which wears it, and so the figure cannot be dispensed with. This is the 'manikin' – Adams himself. Adams does not want readers to read the text in order to learn personal details about him. Rather, he wishes to figure in the text in an impersonal manner, as the vehicle or prop necessary for his 'study of relation', examination of the fit of the garment, to be demonstrated. Reliance on metaphors of costume indicates that identity is to be understood in terms of a self-conscious performance, albeit a performance of reticence and impersonality. Denise Riley's claim that 'irony has to try things on (again, in both senses of that expression) because it is the product of this impersonal integrity' (Riley 2000: 155) suggests that irony is both necessary to, and a consequence of, Adams' use of the manikin. Riley notes that: 'Having something said too many times will make it rise up out of its background, suspended in relief' and that 'it is the presentation and re-presentation of the category to its occupant that produces irony' (2000: 155). It is through the use of irony that Adams questions (but, crucially, refuses to dispense with) the category of 'representative man' and his presentation of himself as one.

Ironically, it is to eighteenth century texts that Adams turns (tilts?), in order to find ways of thinking about identity and autobiography in the late nineteenth and twentieth centuries. This is despite his repeated claims that the world he lives in is one in which traditional models no longer have the same meaning (the child of the seventeenth century cannot play the game of the twentieth). But the 'manikin' he describes is by no means as blank and impersonal as he wishes it to be. The 'toilet of education' that it will be draped in will be tailored for a particular kind of identity; one size, one outfit, does not fit all. The manikin represents the model of selfhood most often represented and valorised in the history of autobiography, emblematised by Adams himself – the white, middle-class, Western male. It is *because* this model of selfhood is privileged, understood as universally representative, that Adams can hide behind the manikin, aspiring to impersonality, while losing none of the authority or the markings of his particular raced, classed and gendered identity (this is ironic, but Adams does not seem to scrutinise it). Clearly, it is the education of young men which interests Adams, and young men for whom his autobiography is presumed to be edifying.

The gap between narrated and narrating selves is central to Adams' autobiographical project, emphasised by his strategy of writing about himself in the third-person. James M. Cox argues that use of the third-person enables Adams to avoid being forced into the metonymic representative move. Whereas the first-person 'I' renders the autobiographer a 'character' (and, for Cox, therefore, alluding to fiction and drama), third-person allows 'a division of the self into two parts, two poles – a past and a present – in which the present self generates the past self as history' (Cox 1971: 270). For Cox, treatment of the self as history is more appropriate for autobiography. Adams' position (and Cox's reading) is complicated by the fact that, in the terms of Adams' analogies, he is manikin *and* tailor, teacher-historian *and* student. If the Adams who is narrated is styled as a student, the Adams who narrates occupies the role of teacher and educator – the historian engaged in 'the study of relation'. And if the lessons of the text are those of continual failure, then Adams' identity as student does not belong to the past (in any case, Cox is too quick to think that history and fiction in autobiography can be easily distinguished). Certainly, it is by referring to himself in the third person that Adams attempts to bridge the gap between living and writing a life (the way in which he chooses to write his autobiography demonstrates the propositions he wishes to demonstrate and prove). By writing about himself in the third person, Adams can illustrate (justify?) his argument that the student is the passive object upon which the 'toilet of education is to be draped'. The passive object of study can be regarded as a victim of circumstance, living in an era in which the education with which he is being fitted is woefully inadequate for the purpose. This also encourages the notion that Adams is not to be considered the subject of his autobiography; so impersonal is he, so much the manikin, that he does not even claim the first-person 'I'.

However, there are at least two further very personal explanations for the effacement of Adams' ego in this text. The twentieth and twenty-first chapters of his autobiography are separated by a 20-year gap, which covers the period from 1871 to 1892. In 1885, Adams' wife, Marion Hooper, committed suicide, and the chronological gap in the text is usually explained by Adams' subsequent grief and unwillingness, or inability, to recount this painful event and its aftermath. Adams' autobiography can be, therefore, characterised as a text of missing (personal) parts. His use of the third-person voice, the eagerness with which he seizes on the device of the manikin, his identities as 'student' and 'historian' (not 'husband' or 'son', say), his insistence that readers should not read the text for personal information about himself – all this makes sense, if Adams does not wish to embark on painful examination of past events. Indeed, these features perhaps provide a 'loophole', allowing Adams to do 'what is needful'; they justify his decision to produce an autobiography with very little of the 'self' in it, one very selective in including incidents from the 'life'.

Self-examination, for Adams, is a difficult exercise. This is seen in his attempt to describe the 'interest' Washington had for him as a child:

> The more he was educated, the less he understood. Slavery struck him in the face; it was a nightmare; a horror; a crime; the sum of all wickedness! Contact made it only more repulsive. He wanted to escape, like the negroes, to free soil. Slave States were dirty, unkempt, poverty-stricken, ignorant, vicious! He had not a thought but repulsion for it; and yet the picture had another side. The May sunshine and shadow had something to do with it; the thickness of foliage and the heavy smells had more; the sense of atmosphere, almost new, had perhaps as much again; and the brooding indolence of a warm climate and a negro population hung in the atmosphere heavier than the

catalpas. The impression was not simple, but the boy liked it: distinctly it remained on his mind as an attraction, almost obscuring Quincy itself. The want of barriers, of pavement, of forms; the looseness; the laziness; the indolent Southern drawl; the pigs in the streets; the negro babies and their mothers with bandanas; the freedom, openness, swagger, of nature and man, soothed his Johnson blood. Most boys would have felt it in the same way, but with him the feeling caught on to an inheritance. The softness of his gentle old grandmother as she lay in bed and chatted with him, did not come from Boston. His aunt was anything rather than Bostonian. He did not wholly come from Boston himself. Though Washington belonged to a different world, and the two worlds could not live together, he was not sure that he enjoyed the Boston world most. Even at twelve years old he could see his own nature no more clearly than he would at twelve hundred, if by accident he should happen to live so long. ([1916] 2008: 42–3)

If there was a moment in the autobiography in which Adams aspires to a Whitman-like project of identification with, and imaginative investment, in others, then this might be it – recording his sense of wonder in the slave state of Boston, he is participant in, and observer of, the scene and actually lays propriety claim to it, in the sense that he calls it an 'inheritance'; something which helps him explain who he is. However, the description of Washington is contradictory and confused. Adams' outrage about slavery is perhaps muted somewhat by the exoticised presentation of African-American life and the further appropriation involved in Adams' claim that the atmosphere of Washington constitutes an 'inheritance'. His excitement about 'the want of barriers, of pavement, of forms' reflects the sense of discovery he feels as an adult, living in an American culture in which previously secure boundaries of place and identity are being uprooted. However, the passage is marked by Adams' reluctance to engage in self-scrutiny. He confesses a failure to understand the complex feelings and identifications he describes. But his confessions of ignorance and bewilderment are often self-disparaging, comic and ironic. Like Thoreau's confession of his inability to write a poem in text which looks like a poem, Adams' repeated confessions of his ignorance work to suggest the opposite; that this is a thoughtful, well-educated man. Adams' retreat from self-scrutiny functions analogously to his refusal to dismiss the world Boston represents (one in which, presumably, barriers, pavements and forms are more securely installed). Much is at stake for Adams, personally, in relinquishing the ideologies and meta-narratives which have organised American culture, prior to the mid-nineteenth and early twentieth centuries.

One way of examining what is at stake for Adams in relinquishing such narratives is revealed by considering that strategy of referring to himself in the third person. This could be a sign of self-aggrandisement, not self-effacement. His conception of himself as a failure – a victim of circumstance – is overdrawn, given the privileged position he occupies. As a member of one of America's most noteworthy families, Adams' life is privileged, marked by opportunities not available to all and untouched by the oppressions determining existence for many in America, during the time in which he lives and writes. Readers may find Adams unsympathetic for these reasons. And, unlike Whitman, Adams does not claim representative status for the purposes of declaring imaginative identification with the nation's citizens as a whole or with its oppressed citizens, in particular. To an extent, this is understandable, given that Adams' construction of himself as a 'historian' means that his thoughts on women, African-Americans and people of other nationalities reflect a (supposedly objective) tendency to conceive of people as representative 'types', objects of study, not individuals. Here, for example, is Adams considering the plight of American women:

> The American woman at her best – like most other women – exerted great charm on the man, but not the charm of a primitive type. She appeared as the result of a long series of discards, and her chief interest lay in what she had discarded. When closely watched, she seemed making a violent effort to follow the man, who had turned his mind and hand to mechanics. The typical American man had his hand on the lever and his eye on a curve in his road; his living depended on keeping up an average speed of forty miles an hour, tending always to become sixty, eighty, or a hundred, and he could not admit emotions or anxieties or subconscious distractions, more than he could admit whiskey or drugs, without breaking his neck. He could not run his machine and a woman too; he must leave her, even though his wife, to find her own way, and all the world saw her trying to find her way by imitating him. ([1916] 2008: 371–2)

While Adams does not place faith in evolutionary theory as an explanatory model, his claim that the American woman is not to be confused with a 'primitive type' reveals how he can participate in a logic which reinforces certain hierarchies of race and gender in American culture.

His emphasis on 'discards' and his description of women as machines run by men reveals the themes Adams gives much thought to in his text – the reification of individual identity and the fracturing of relations of many kinds, caused by ever-increasing industrialisation in modernity. But Adams' frequent failure to interrogate those hierarchies of race and gender in American culture mean that his 'study of relation' is not as radical as it could be. John Carlos Rowe argues that the text 'reveals as it protects, explains as it mystifies, "confesses" as it represses some of the most significant personal and historical records of American modernity' (1996: 2). Adams is astute in documenting the causes and consequences of the break-up of grand narratives of history and progress and is sceptical about whether those grand narratives had, or can have, value. But he is also, clearly, regretful about their passing. His interrogation of the world in which he lives has limits. In general, his text does not argue for, or celebrate, a politics of inclusion. In general, it does not reveal empathy for those categorised as 'other' in his society, nor does it represent their 'interests'. He is perhaps unwilling to fully consider a world broken up into smaller parts, as this would undermine the privilege attached to his own nation, race, gender and class – privileges which clearly still have value for him.

Given Adams' frequent refusal to engage in personal revelation and examination, and the importance the identity of 'historian' holds for him, it is all the more vital to answer Howard Horwitz's question: 'Why did autobiography initially seem to Adams the suitable genre to convey his dynamic theory of history?' (Horwitz, in Rowe 1996: 119). This necessitates considering the identity of 'historian'. Jeremy D. Popkin offers a useful discussion of the relationship between history and autobiography. He argues that historical and autobiographical projects share certain features: both involve study of the past and the setting down of an account of the past on paper; both aim (or claim) to tell the truth about the past; both may make use of documents – such as letters or birth certificates – in order to verify their claims. Popkin also makes it clear that historical and autobiographical projects are very different. When a historian sets down an account of the past, he or she usually writes at a distance from his or her material. An autobiographer, however, is, by necessity, intimately involved with the events he or she recounts (of course, we should question the presumed 'objectivity' of the historian here). Autobiographers have no need to rely on documents to the degree that historians do; the main resource for an autobiographer is *memory*, and not all memories can be verified, documented or proven. For example, readers often only have an autobiographer's testimony that he or she thought or felt a certain way at a specific time. It is this final characteristic, in particular, Popkin argues, which causes many historians to be uncomfortable with locating autobiography within the discipline of 'history'; for many, the fact that an autobiographer is seemingly not so beholden to 'the facts' means that autobiography belongs more properly to the genre of 'fiction'. Further, historians are often sceptical of first-person narrative accounts, in the sense that they study these narratives for biases, which undermine a narrator's reliability (Popkin 2005: 9–16).

In *The Education of Henry Adams*, Adams arrives at what he calls a 'dynamic theory of history'. He takes, as his starting point, 'progress as the development and economy of forces'. He adds that: 'It defines force as anything that does, or helps to do work. Man is a force; so is the sun; so is a mathematical point, though without dimensions or known existence' ([1916] 2008: 395). Ultimately, though, Adams is forced to concede that there is no unity or certainty to be found in the world and the course of history, hence, his growing reliance on the concept of 'multiplicity'. The only certainty Adams seems to adhere to is that there can be no certainty; he finds some order and consolation in the fact that he can say that there is no order:

> Man commonly begs the question again by taking for granted that he captures the forces. A dynamic theory, assigning attractive forces to opposing bodies in proportion to the law of mass, takes for granted that the forces of nature capture man. The sum of force attracts; the feeble atom or molecule called man is attracted; he suffers education or growth; he is the sum of the forces that attract him; his body and his thought are alike their product; the movement of the forces controls the progress of his mind, since he can know nothing but the motions which impinge on his senses, whose sum makes education. ([1916] 2008: 395)

Here, and throughout his autobiography, Adams illustrates Riley's argument that 'irony's question is no longer of how you tolerate or admire uncertainty, but how you tolerate or admire knowing, as this tips danger-ously towards knowingness' (2000: 147). For Adams (ironically, given the aims of his text), the solution is found *not* in relation: 'Every student would, like the private secretary, answer for himself alone' ([1916] 2008: 142). This may be a generous act, in that it grants readers the capacity to arrive at their own understandings and might even be understood as Adams' recognition of the unsustainable category of 'representative man'. But in discussing the affinities between irony and the echo, Riley claims that 'no echo, being automatic, can knowingly provoke any intelligible response, let alone constitute one in itself' (2000: 156). If so, *The Education of Henry Adams* may communicate a 'strictly solitary ethic of performance' (2000: 157).

Gertrude Stein's *The Autobiography of Alice B. Toklas* (1933) makes its problematic status as autobiography clear from its title. The individual whose autobiography the text supposedly comprises (Alice B. Toklas) is not the individual who authors that text (Gertrude Stein). Anna Linzie notes the text's 'controversial status as a mock autobiography' (Linzie 2006: 1) – a potentially useful label, which alludes to the sense of play so central to the text. Comparing Stein's and Adams' texts is a useful exercise, as both texts share an ironic inquiry into the nature of identity and subjectivity in modernity – an inquiry facilitated by the strategy of portraying the subject by means other than the first person 'I'. They can be understood as partaking in an autobiographical tradition which Richard Hardack describes as 'ventriloquism, or third-person representation of the self' (Hardack, in Bak and Krabbendam 1998: 16). Hardack further understands this as a particularly American tradition, claiming that:

> in the last several hundred years, American autobiographies of a certain genre have gradually but self-consciously turned away from the representation of a linear self and moved toward a staging of memory and self-identity as fictions of alienation and reification. (1998: 16)

Adams' and Stein's texts are among autobiographies he identifies as 'structured around the pretense of biography, or perhaps the biographies of missing persons' (1998: 16).

Hardack's claim has merit, but it is also problematic. While his sense that he is only looking at one tradition of autobiography is commendable, his desire to, nonetheless, chart a history of American autobiography seems doomed to inevitable oversimplifications and exclusions. Exactly what is meant by a 'linear self' is unclear and, in any case, is obviously not evidenced by Stein's text. Like the label of 'mock autobiography', Hardack's eagerness to place Stein within a tradition of American autobiography does a disservice to the complexity of the text. By locating

Stein in a 'tradition' with Adams, Hardack does not sufficiently acknowledge the difference between the two texts. Stein's text *is* structured around 'the pretense of biography'. And, certainly, the text can be understood as 'mock autobiography', in that it critiques what is meant by autobiography; in particular, like all the texts discussed in this chapter, it troubles the valorisation of the representative self in autobiography. Female, Jewish, in a homosexual relationship, an American expatriate in Paris, Stein is no representative man. By writing her autobiography in an unconventional manner, Stein emphasises how that conventional form does not enable an accurate representation of her experience (and, further, may make it difficult for her voice and experience to be recognised). Linzie argues that Stein's text '[defies] expectations of normative gender and sexuality (*be straight! straighten up!*) as well as the protocol of autobiographical discourse (*tell it to me straight!*)' (2006: 21–2).

For Gilmore, *The Autobiography of Alice B. Toklas* constitutes an example of 'autobiographics':

I offer the term autobiographics to describe those elements of self-representation which are not bound by a philosophical definition of the self derived from Augustine, not content with a literary theory of autobiography, those elements that instead mark a location in a text where self-invention, self-discovery and self-representation emerge within the technologies of autobiography – namely, those legalistic, literary, social, and ecclesiastical discourses of truth and identity through which the subject of autobiography is produced. Autobiographics, as a description of self-representation and as a reading practice, is concerned with interruptions and eruptions, with resistance and contradiction as strategies of self-representation.

A text's autobiographics consist of the following elements in self-representational writing, or writing that emphasises the autobiographical I: an emphasis on writing itself as constitutive of autobiographical identity, discursive contradictions in the representation of identity (rather than unity), the name as a potential site of experimentation rather than contractual sign of identity, and the effects of the gendered connection of word and body. Autobiographics gives initial conceptual precedence to positioning the subject, to recognising the shifting sands of identity on which theories of autobiography build, and to describing "identity" and the networks of identification. An exploration of a text's autobiographics allows us to recognise that the I is multiply coded in a range of discourses: it is the site of multiple solicitations, multiple markings of 'identity,' multiple figurations of agency. Thus, autobiographics avoids the terminal questions of genre and close delimitation and offers a way, instead, to ask: Where is the autobiographical? What constitutes its representation? (1994: 42)

Gilmore's analysis of autobiographics, and her description of its features, offers an invaluable framework for reading autobiographies, especially those by women which have suffered from being misread and sidelined, because their subjects (the author who writes, the life described) do not fit (imitate) the model presented by that of the representative man. However, although Gilmore's work is taking issue with the work of Philippe Lejeune, in particular (whose work will be discussed in the following chapter), she, too, appears to be engaging in the project of attempting to 'name the parts' of a particular kind of autobiography. This leads to an important point: as vital as Gilmore's work is, it is, also, too narrow in its understanding of 'autobiographics'. Her analysis is, perhaps, too quick to dismiss the autobiographies of white males and representative men as identical and, therefore, reflects a simplistic acceptance of that representative status (hopefully, the discussions of Thoreau, Whitman and Adams so far should reveal that this is not the case). In a related point, the features she describes as comprising 'autobiographics' probably need to be moved from margin to centre. Gilmore thinks of all the autobiographies she analyses as demonstrating 'autobiographics' as fringe, 'limit-cases' (2001: 7). But *any* autobiography can, theoretically, be read in relation to the questions she poses above. Additionally, it is (ironically) the case that the autobiographies Gilmore discusses, in their status as experiments in the study of relation, are much more truly (normatively?) representative of what autobiography is and does. It is the autobiographies of the 'representative men' which are 'limit-cases', comprising only one subset of autobiography. To this extent, labelling Stein's text as 'mock autobiography' does it a disservice, because it continues to privilege a particular kind of autobiography (that of the representative man) and implies that her text is a shadow, a distorted version of a fixed autobiographical template. While it is true that Stein's text does need to be understood in relation to that autobiographical tradition, another way of characterising that relationship needs to be found.

One of the most obvious ways in which *The Autobiography of Alice B. Toklas* 'mocks' the conventions of a certain kind of autobiography is seen in its portrayal of identity as constructed via relationship. The text declares itself to be Alice's autobiography, yet readers encounter a knot of representation and authorship, in which Alice appears to be presenting a biography of Stein, and, yet, it is Stein who impersonates Alice, who represents Stein. This challenges any simplistic understanding of what truth, reference and identity mean, in relation to this, and any, autobiography. It is, indeed, a strategy by which, in Hardack's terms, Stein stages 'self-identity as [a] fiction of alienation and reification' (Hardack, in Bak and Krabbendam 1998: 16). But there is more. Stein rejects the (masculine) model of identity as self-determining and isolate and emphasises that – for her, at least – identity is relational, a product of interactions with others. The 'other' most central to Stein's sense of self, then, is Alice, and it is fitting that some critics have understood the text to comprise a love letter to Alice (Linzie 2006: 56). It would therefore be appropriate to think of Stein's text, too, as a gift. But, in that case, who gives and who receives the gift? Linzie claims that while there is a tendency to regard the book as a gift from Stein to Alice, perhaps it is 'the other way round' (2006: 57). And, as always, this is only one – generous – reading of the text. Readers may feel that Stein is engaging in a dubious appropriation of another's voice, a betrayal of trust and privacy (one way to think of this might be to say that Stein privileges writing a life over the ethical considerations of living a life). The relationship between Stein and Toklas is fraught with ethical and political complications, regarding its performance of traditional gendered roles. Alice's repeated reference to the fact that she commonly sits with the 'wives of geniuses' ([1933] 2001: 18) describes a gendered binary, in which Stein is identified as 'masculine' and 'genius', and the category of 'wife' seems to foreclose an identity as 'genius'. It is true that Stein and Toklas' relationship exposes the artificiality of understanding certain behaviours and identities as 'masculine' and 'feminine', and this is where the text is powerful in its exposure and questioning of the logic which grants some (autobiographical) subjects more authority than others. But the fact that Stein and Toklas's relationship replicates a hierarchy in which Toklas's role is that of muse, housekeeper, the person who creates the time and space for Stein to do the (seemingly more important) work of artistic production, is troubling. Indeed, Carolyn A. Barros argues that Stein 'never gives the *Autobiography* over to the reader' and that Alice (but, importantly, as represented by Stein) 'makes us listen to the voices she wants us to hear and to look at the portraits she wants us to see' (1999: 201).

All of these tensions are expressed in the text's autobiographical occasion, which, unusually, is revealed not at the beginning of the text, but in the very final paragraphs. Despite the claim, below, that an autobiography of Stein is 'impossible', the text nonetheless attempts to provide such a thing:

> For some time now many people, and publishers, have been asking Gertrude Stein to write her autobiography and she had always replied, not possibly.
>
> She began to tease me and say that I should write my autobiography. Just think, she would say, what a lot of money you would make. She then began to invent titles for my autobiography. My Life With The Great, Wives of Geniuses I Have Sat With, My Twenty-Five Years With Gertrude Stein.
>
> Then she began to get serious and say, but really seriously you ought to write your autobiography. Finally I promised that if during the summer I could find time I would write my autobiography.
>
> When Ford Madox Ford was editing the Transatlantic Review he once said to Gertrude Stein, I am a pretty good writer and a pretty good editor and a pretty good businessman but I find it difficult to be all these at once.
>
> I am a pretty good housekeeper and a pretty good gardener and a pretty good needlewoman and a pretty good secretary and a pretty good editor and a pretty good vet for dogs and I have to do them all at once and I find it difficult to add being a pretty good author.
>
> About six weeks ago Gertrude Stein said, it does not look to me as if you were ever going to write that autobiography. You know what I am going to do. I am going to write it for you. I am going to write it as simply as Defoe did the autobiography of Robinson Crusoe. And she has and this is it. ([1933] 2001: 271–2)

The text finally reveals what the reader probably already knows – that Stein is 'ventriloquising' Alice, and Alice is functioning as the ventriloquist's dummy (Linzie 2006: 60). This revelation allows Stein to finally claim authorship, something not claimed at the beginning (this would seem to be because much of the work of the text is to deconstruct how the role of 'author' has been gendered, and to show how difficult it might be for Stein to lay claim to such an identity). These final paragraphs do support that reading of the text as a gift or a love letter, acknowledging the work which Alice does and her vital role in Stein's life. Particularly intriguing are the final two lines: 'I am going to write it as simply as Defoe did the autobiography of Robinson Crusoe. And she has and this is it'. A comparison is made between this text and a male-authored fiction – a fiction which takes the form of an autobiography. It is a comparison which both acknowledges and ironically engages with Couser's point that 'the modern novel emerged as an imitation of life writing' (2012: 9–10). That male-authored fiction describes a character who can be understood both as representing that masculine model of isolate identity – Crusoe lives on an island – and a model of identity found through an ethically compromised relationship (with Man Friday). Parodying the metonymic gesture which enables the installation of the representative man, Defoe's text stands in for, but is then replaced with, *The Autobiography of Alice B. Toklas*, at the same time as Stein replaces Toklas as author of the text. The final line thus takes on the qualities of one of Sedgwick's explicit performative utterances, in that it seems to do what it describes – it transfers the role of author from Toklas to Stein; it declares that the autobiography is completed and achieved (the final line completes the autobiography). Specifically, the performative utterance it comprises is a promise. Toklas promises to write her own autobiography, but cannot. Stein ensures that Alice's promise is kept, by carrying it out for her. But the promise is also broken, because Stein keeps Alice's promise.

Riley argues that:

> irony, once achieved, will always sidle away from anyone's ownership. A public irony must flourish, for the sake of the political and ethical vigour of language; lurking inside a self-categorisation, ideally it can inspect the limits of any expansionist identification, can check hyperbole, can puncture any overblown claims from within to arrive at a sounder measure of them. It guarantees a grasp of proportion. (2000: 162–3)

All the autobiographers examined in this chapter 'inspect the limits' of two categories: that of 'representative man' and of 'autobiography'. In different ways, they employ contradiction, paradox and, especially, irony, as a means of tilting those categories, revealing their foundations to be less than solid – as Riley claims, such strategies have the effect of exposing '[a category's] historicity and fragility by isolating it as both real enough yet also as an artefact, eminently questionable' (2000: 162–3). While emphasising the 'study of relations', each autobiographer *only* unsettles these categories. Thoreau, Whitman, Adams and Stein are reluctant to surrender the privileges, freedoms and authority which attend presenting oneself as 'representative' or one's text as 'autobiography', especially if, as in Stein's case, those privileges, freedoms and authority were never granted in the first place.

PART TWO

Contemporary Subjects

CHAPTER 3

Relating Ethics to Genre

The pair of ancient, stunted apricot trees yielded ancient, stunted apricots. What was the meaning hung from that depend. The sweet aftertaste of artichokes. The lobes of autobiography. Even a minor misadventure, a bumped fender or a newsstand without newspapers, can "ruin the entire day," but a child cries and laughs without rift. The sky droops straight down. I lapse, hypnotised by the flux and reflux of the waves. (Hejinian 1987: 27–8)

Throughout Lyn Hejinian's prose poem, *My Life*, and illustrated clearly in the passage above, *relations* are central to the text's conceptualisation of identity, the individual life described and the act of writing autobiography (*auto/bios/graphe*: self, life, writing). *My Life* requires the reader to determine the relationships between individuals and their environment described in the lines above, and the relationships between the apparently disconnected sentences – 'What was the meaning hung from that depend'. In so clearly bestowing the task of interpreting the autobiography upon the reader, Hejinian's text unsettles assumptions that the author is the privileged site of authority, suggesting that the role of reader is of equal, if not greater, importance. And rather than conceiving of the self as a sovereign, isolate, self-determining entity (corresponding to the Enlightenment-influenced model of selfhood historically privileged by many white, Western male autobiographers and critics), identity in *My Life* is provisional, formed by relationships with other people, other things.

Hejinian's text might stand as representative of an autobiography influenced by (some) features of post-structural philosophical thought, which had a marked influence on the construction and study of autobiography from the 1970s (and, of course, this claim of the 'representative' status of Hejinian's text is made in full awareness of the problems of according any text 'representative' status, which has been discussed in previous chapters). The insights of structuralist and post-structuralist theory pertain to new understandings of the self and the author as no longer discrete, unified and autonomous entities, but, instead, as products of various sign systems in specific cultures and historical moments. These insights place conventional understandings of autobiography under particular pressure, because, as G. Thomas Couser explains, the authority of autobiography 'has traditionally been grounded in a verifiable relationship between a text and an extratextual referent (the writer's self, or life)' (1989: vii). The dilemma for Couser, and for many other critics and writers of autobiography who engage with post-structural thought, then, is how to write, read and interpret autobiography (understood to present a truthful account of a person's life) in the absence of certainty about what identity or truth entails. Linda Anderson discusses the consequence of this problematic situation:

> So far as autobiography is concerned, the usefulness of poststructuralist theory for our understanding of it continues to be debated. The argument that texts can have political or historical effect revives the question of referentiality or truth, without necessarily returning us to the same place. Indeed the notion of multiple locations, both as contexts of reading and positionings for the subject, becomes one of the ways autobiography has offered itself as a site for new theoretical and critical insights. (2011: 15)

The attention currently given to understandings of identity as relational in contemporary autobiography, as well as in critical studies of autobiography and life writing, suggests that this offers one of several possible ways to register and explore, even perhaps to overcome, the difficulties Couser notes. A consideration of identity as relational, therefore, also provides one way of ensuring that autobiographies (and criticism of autobiography) informed by post-structuralist thought do, indeed, refuse to 'return us to the same place', in Anderson's terms. Notably, Anderson's suggestion that autobiography 'has offered itself' as a productive site for examining questions of referentiality and truth contains the suggestion that autobiography can be considered as a gift; that gift being its capacity to uproot the reader, to take him or her to a different 'place'. For example, in Hejinian's passage above, everyday existence is comprised of multiple interactions and encounters (a bumped fender can ruin one's day). Hejinian's passage suggests, in fact, that acquisition of adult identity entails the capacity to make ethical distinctions, to acknowledge and negotiate the relationship between laughter and tears, something the child cannot do; he or she 'cries and laughs without rift'. The 'truth' of the passage is conceived as partial (that is, subjective), fluid, multiple and provisional, approaching the speaker's grasp, only to recede again and again, like 'the flux and reflux of the waves'. The speaker in the passage above acknowledges this situation and appears to accept it, even as she repeatedly attempts to grapple with its difficulties.

Paul John Eakin's work provides an illustrative example of the current attention given to the relational by critics of autobiography. Eakin has written several critical works on autobiography and is one of its most engaging and thoughtful theorists. That he has clearly felt the need to revisit the subject of autobiography several times throughout his career reflects his constantly evolving understanding of the genre, supporting Anderson's point that the 'multiple locations' occupied by a reader present multiple ways of theorising autobiography. Relational identity is given significant attention in Eakin's most recent critical works. The first of his works to address the topic, *How Our Lives Become Stories* (1999), reveals awareness of post-structuralist thought and its implications for autobiography:

> We tend to think of autobiography as a literature of the first person, but the subject of autobiography to which the pronoun 'I' refers is neither singular nor first, and we do well to demystify its claims. Why do we so easily forget that the first person of autobiography is truly plural in its origins and subsequent formation? Because autobiography promotes an illusion of self-determination: *I* write my story, *I* say who I am, *I* create my self. The myth of autonomy dies hard, and autobiography criticism has not yet fully addressed the extent to which the self is defined by – and lives in terms of – its relations with others. (Eakin 1999: 43)

Eakin is correct, but there is a sense that his insights are belated. As he notes, to focus on identity as relational is not to address something new in autobiography, but to acknowledge the importance of a concept which has *always* been present in autobiography. Autobiographies are always about relationships. In fact, it is by deliberately focusing on relationships that autobiographies by women and non-white authors have questioned and deconstructed the 'myth of self-determination' Eakin refers to, exposing its rootedness in ideologies which privilege white male identity. They also prioritise relationships in order to promote the ethical and political agendas of their texts (see, for example, Culley 1992; Egan 1999; Moore-Gilbert 2009). What Eakin is referring to, then, is a shift in perception. As Amy Culley and Rebecca Styler note, in their editorial for a *Life Writing* special issue on 'Lives in relation', 'relational selfhood' is now foregrounded in studies of autobiography and life writing, whereas, previously, it was considered (if considered) as a strategy or practice of women's life writing, in particular (2011: 1). There are several factors to note here. Firstly, because understandings of identity as relational have *always* been present in autobiography, any claims of a radical change in the way autobiography is written or theorised, as a consequence of post-structural thought, should be treated with caution. That is, many autobiographies written and published before 1970 – itself a date that should not be understood strictly – exemplify some of the features and insights of texts informed by post-structuralism. Franklin's text, for example, could be read as presenting a version of identity as performative and, to that extent, suggesting that there is no authentic 'truth' of the self. Similarly, many autobiographies published after 1970 reveal the continued influence of Enlightenment models of identity and continue to prioritise what Eakin calls the 'illusion of self-determination' (an example might be Lance Armstrong's autobiography, discussed in the following chapter). Finally, Eakin's focus on relational identity indicates that it has become a topic of concern and interest to critics who previously may have privileged that 'myth of autonomy' and the ideologies and values it propagates. What, then, are the implications for autobiographies written by female and non-white writers of this sudden appropriation of the relational as central to *all* autobiography?

Hejinan's enigmatic phrase – 'the lobes of autobiography' – is illustrative, in relation to the points above. What can 'the lobes of autobiography' possibly mean? It constitutes an intertextual reference to *Walden*, in which Thoreau meditates on the word 'lobe':

> No wonder that the earth expresses itself outwardly in leaves, it so labors with the idea inwardly. The atoms have already learned this law, and are pregnant by it. The overhanging leaf sees here its prototype. *Internally*, whether in the globe or animal body, it is a moist thick *lobe*, a word especially applicable to the liver and lungs and the *leaves* of fat, (λειβω, *labor*, *lapsus*, to flow or slip downward, a lapsing; λοβος, *globus*, lobe, globe; also lap, flap, and many other words,) *externally* a dry thin *leaf*, even as the *f* and *v* are a pressed and dried *b*.

The radicals of lobe are *lb*, the soft mass of the *b* (single lobed, or **B**, double lobed,) with a liquid *l* behind it pressing it forward. In globe, *glb*, the guttural *g* adds to the meaning the capacity of the throat. The feathers and wings of birds are still drier and thinner leaves. Thus, also, you pass from the lumpish grub in the earth to the airy and fluttering butterfly. The very globe continually transcends and translates itself, and becomes winged in its orbit. (273)

In *My Life*, the meaning of the word 'lobes' is uncertain, because it lacks reference, whereas for Thoreau, the word refers to so much that it threatens to lose its meaning. In Hejinian's usage, it is unclear whether 'lobes' refers to the body (lobes of the brain, ears?) or to the natural world (leaves?). Certainly, her passage focuses on the natural world – trees, artichokes, apricots. For Thoreau, though, the word refers to both, and the fact that it does so illustrates the interconnectedness of all things (he is at pains to show how the visual appearance and shape of the letters comprising the word 'lobe', dictating the sound of its utterance, assist in communicating the word's meaning). Whereas Hejinian leaves the work of determining the meaning of 'lobes' to the reader, Thoreau informs readers of its meaning, in exhaustive detail. These differences may indicate the different historical and gendered locations of each autobiographer. Thoreau's authoritative account claims mastery and authority over the interconnected world he describes. For him, letters are 'pressed and dried' ([1854] 2008: 273). This calls to mind the practice of preserving flowers or leaves for scientific study, suggesting that Thoreau's autobiography records his life and world in a similar spirit. In naming the parts of his world and including them within his text, he collects them, makes them his own. While Hejinian's text does not posit the author as the privileged authority, the place where some singular truth or meaning resides, *My Life* shares that preoccupation with naming, itemising, documenting the world. Her reference to 'lobes' suggests that readers are to puzzle over the relation of her text to Thoreau's; where *My Life* is to be located within traditions of American autobiography.

Most compellingly, Hejinian's 'lobes of autobiography' figures autobiography as a *thing*, as a material, even living, object. It suggests that autobiography should be considered an assemblage of, with relations between, multiple parts. If autobiography (both individual autobiographies and autobiography more broadly) is an assemblage of parts, then the naming of parts, the relations between them, and the process of assemblage are puzzles for both author and reader to determine, preferably, Hejinan's text implies, in collaboration. The proximity of the references to autobiography and the description of eating food ('the sweet taste of artichokes') imply that autobiography might be something to be consumed by readers. These associations, provoked by the phrase 'the lobes of autobiography', counter the conventional exclusion or devaluing of the body in models of identity and in autobiography, and they resist any coherent, formulaic definition of autobiography.

In order to further draw out the theme of the relational in autobiography, and to expand upon issues raised by the discussion above, this chapter will first explore Philippe Lejeune's famous essay, 'The autobiographical pact', first published in 1973, which can be understood as a response to some of the challenges that post-structuralist thought poses for autobiography. It will then offer readings of two autobiographical texts – Maxine Hong Kingston's *Woman Warrior* (1977) and Art Spiegelman's *Maus* (1996). These texts explore an understanding of identity as relational, to the extent that understanding either text as 'autobiography' is extremely fraught. As the autobiographies of non-white subjects, they can stand as representative of one significant feature of critical studies of autobiography published after 1970. Sidonie Smith and Julia Watson note a tendency in critical work from this period to 'focus increasingly on [...] other stories of Americanisation among populations dominated and spoken for by the myth of the American melting pot' (2010: 106). Anderson notes that:

> The idea that autobiography can become 'the text of the oppressed', articulating through one person's experience, experiences which may be representative of a particular marginalised group, is an important one: autobiography becomes both a way of testifying to oppression and empowering the subject through their cultural inscription and recognition. (2011: 97)

While Smith, Watson and Anderson's comments are correct, it must be noted that subjects belonging to these 'other', 'spoken for' groups did not wait for the advent of post-structural theory in order to write autobiography, and that the aim of writing as a means of 'testifying to oppression' has been present in autobiography from its beginnings (slave narratives are an obvious example). Rather, as a consequence of understanding that, in Eakin's terms, the pronoun 'I' is 'neither singular nor first' and of remembering that 'the first person of autobiography is truly plural in its origins and subsequent formation', the voices of subjects who are not white, male and middle-class (not 'representative men') are more easily heard (1999: 43).

Lejeune's 'The autobiographical pact' attempts to answer the complex question with which it opens: 'Is it possible to define autobiography?' (Lejeune, in Eakin 1989: 3). The many critiques of the claims advanced in that essay – including Lejeune's re-examination of the question in further essays, most notably, 'The autobiographical pact (bis)' (1982), and subsequent book-length studies – indicate that he did not find a satisfactory answer. Like many critics of autobiography, such as Eakin, he continually returns to the topic. Nonetheless, this early essay remains indispensable for students of autobiography, firstly, because of its limitations, and, secondly, because of its theory of the autobiographical 'pact' or 'contract'. Lejeune's narrow definition of autobiography constitutes one significant limitation. And while his essay does seem aware of the importance of relations of many kinds to autobiography, it does not examine the implications of this in detail. In particular, the essay does not sufficiently examine a vital element of understanding relationships as central to autobiography, pertaining to what might be called 'the ethics of life writing' and which can be understood in relation to a question Eakin asks in another of his critical studies: 'What is the good of life writing, and how, exactly, can it do harm?' (2004: 1).

As noted in the introduction to this study, Lejeune's definition of autobiography is frequently cited by critics, if only in order to refuse it. Lejeune attempts to formulate a working definition of autobiography – a kind of 'naming of parts'. According to Lejeune, autobiography is a 'retrospective prose narrative written by a real person concerning his own existence, where the focus is his individual life, in particular the story of his personality' (Lejeune, in Eakin 1989: 4). Critical scholarship – studies of autobiographies by female and non-white subjects, in particular – has made abundantly clear the limitations of nearly every aspect of this definition, which have been discussed in the introduction of this textbook. While Lejeune has not specifically addressed some of these objections, he has acknowledged, in 'The autobiographical pact (bis)', that the prescriptive, dogmatic nature of his definition is problematic (120–1).

In 'The autobiographical pact', Lejeune cites two 'conditions', which he insists must be satisfied, in order for a text to be autobiography. The author's name must refer to a real person, and it must be identical with the text's narrator and with its principal character. Lejeune claims that these conditions are 'a question of all or nothing' and repeats: 'here, there is neither transition nor latitude. An identity is, or is not' (5). This is simply wrong. Or is it? Stein's *The Autobiography of Alice B. Toklas* does not meet these conditions, and it is worth considering the postmodern fictions of a writer like Paul Auster, which include characters that bear the name of the author, but cannot be understood as autobiography. If a reader understands Stein's text as autobiography, then Lejeune is wrong. If a reader believes Lejeune's criteria to be correct, then Stein's text is not autobiography. To compound this complexity, Lejeune's essay contradicts itself. It acknowledges that such 'all or nothing' formulations are impossible: 'To succeed in giving a clear and complete formula of autobiography would be, in reality, to fail' (30). Lejeune's essay occupies a contradictory position shared by many studies of autobiography, only exacerbated from the 1970s onwards; it reveals desires to define, totalise, circumscribe, master and name just what autobiography is, even as it acknowledges that such a totalising enterprise cannot succeed. The useful, if unintended (because not explicitly communicated), message of Lejeune's work on autobiography is that *every* autobiography can be considered as an exception to (refusal to obey) the 'rule' (his description of autobiography as a truthful account of an individual life, authored by that individual), which none observes.

Lejeune's notion of the 'pact' or 'contract' addresses questions of truth and genre, in relation to the task of reading autobiography. In a valuable observation, Lejeune emphasises the importance of the author as 'a person who writes and publishes. Straddling the world-beyond-the-text and the text, he is the connection between the two' (11). That is, the author writes an autobiography, creates a text, is *in* the text, but the author is also a real person living in the world. This leads to one of Lejeune's central claims:

> As opposed to all forms of fiction, biography and autobiography are *referential* texts: exactly like scientific or historical discourse, they claim to provide information about a 'reality' exterior to the text, and so to submit to a test of *verification*. Their aim is not simple verisimilitude, but resemblance to the truth. Not 'the effect of the real,' but the image of the real. All referential texts thus entail what I will call a 'referential pact,' implicit or explicit, in which are included a definition of the field of the real that is involved and a statement of the modes and the degree of resemblance to which the text lays claim. (22)

One of the greatest failures of the essay is its lack of consideration of
the implications of this claim (the question of reference, in relation to
fictional texts, also surely merits more thought). As Linda Haverty Rugg
notes, in her excellent study of the relations between autobiography and
photography, not only is the question of reference in autobiography
highly problematic, but it could be argued that it is *because* autobiography is a referential genre that post-structural insights are not necessarily easily accommodated by it:

> Autobiography, like photography, refers to something beyond itself;
> namely, the autobiographical or photographed subject. But both
> autobiography and photography participate in a system of signs that
> we have learned to read – at one level – as highly indeterminate and
> unreliable. Below that level of doubt rests, in some persons, the desire
> to accept the image or the text as a readable reference to a (once-)
> living person. (Haverty Rugg 1997: 13)

The referential quality of autobiography underpins Lejeune's claim
that '[a]utobiography, (narrative recounting the life of the author)
supposes that there is *identity of name* between the author (such as he
figures, by his name, on the cover), the narrator of the story, and the
character who is being talked about' (12). He explains how that 'identity
of name' between author, narrator and protagonist can be established
in two ways: '*implicitly*', where the title or other material makes it clear
that the 'I' spoken of in the text is the author; and '*in an obvious way*',
where the author's name on the cover and the name of the protagonist
and narrator match (14). For Lejeune: 'It is thus in relation to the proper
name that we are able to situation the problems of autobiography' (11),
and 'What defines autobiography for the one who is reading is above
all a contract of identity that is sealed by the proper name. And this is
true also for the one who is writing the text' (19). If a text satisfies one
of the two ways above, in which identity in name is established between
writer, protagonist and narrator, then we have an autobiography. But
Lejeune's argument that the questions of truth, reference and definition in autobiography coalesce in the 'proper name' is problematic.
Feminist critics (Gilmore, in particular) have identified the patriarchal
privileges inscribed in the 'proper name' and have shown how they, and
Lejeune's understanding of autobiography, legitimate a particular model
of identity, power and truth, based on the tendency to figure 'the one
who is writing the text' as male (Gilmore 1994: 81–2). Again, Stein is

a good example: *The Autobiography of Alice B. Toklas* either breaks the terms of Lejeune's contract or simply disregards them.

The essay's indecision regarding use of the terms 'contract' and 'pact', together with the fact that it posits several contracts and pacts, is surely indicative of confusion and suggests that these ideas require further examination. And they have merit. Two suggestions can be made. Rather than thinking about autobiography as contractual, it might be useful to think about autobiography as *transactional*. Whereas contracts suggest finalised legal agreements, highlighting the importance of transactions to autobiography foregrounds the fact that crucial to the production and reception of autobiography are relations of exchange (give and take) between writer and reader. It also emphasises that autobiographies are material objects, which participate in economies of exchange. Secondly, displacing Lejeune's prioritisation of a legal framework, in favour of an ethical one, is beneficial – indeed, much of contemporary theory and criticism on autobiography can be understood as engaging in this project of displacement. In so doing, it is particularly indebted to Gilmore's work. In Haverty Rugg's observation (reading Lejeune) that: '[s]elfhood is apparently more a matter of faith (however one defines that) than proof' (1997: 11), the word 'selfhood' could easily be replaced with 'truth'. Lejeune, and many readers, treat truth in autobiography as if it can be verified or measured. That such an understanding continues to be prevalent, despite post-structuralist claims about the relativity or impossibility of truth, is reflected in the fact that autobiographies often generate scandal (and the possibility of legal suits) when autobiographers are believed to have lied in their texts. For example, Binjamin Wilkomirski's autobiography, *Fragments: Memories of a Wartime Childhood* (1995), was eventually withdrawn from publication, when it transpired that its author was not a Holocaust survivor, as the text declared; James Frey's *A Million Little Pieces* (2003) generated controversy, when some details of the text were revealed to be exaggerated.

Understanding autobiography as 'transactional' might help to emphasise the fact that the 'truth' of autobiography resides substantially in the reader, who trusts that the writer is telling the truth. Lejeune's essay is notable for its claim that he attempts to define autobiography from the perspective of the reader (4). Reading autobiography involves some kind of relationship (primarily ethical, rather than legal, though) between author and reader. Implicit in many scandals about truth in autobiographies is a sense of betrayal on the part of readers, who censure the autobiographer for morally dubious behaviour. This sense of betrayal is as important as any desire to prove the truth in law. Eakin argues that: 'When life writers fail to tell the truth, then, they do more than violate a literary convention governing nonfiction as a genre: they disobey a moral imperative' (Eakin 2004: 2–3).

I would prefer to think of 'autobiographical promises', rather than the 'autobiographical pact'. These promises certainly need *not* imply agreement between autobiographer and reader about what the truth entails (that is, about how the promises are made and kept). And it is precisely in how an autobiographer negotiates relations with others that readers can begin to ascertain whether, and how, an autobiography may do good or harm. Embedded within the notion of autobiography as a transactional genre, then, are the suggestions that autobiography partakes of some of the qualities of the both the gift and the promise. In their study of life narratives and human rights, Sidonie Smith and Kay Schaeffer describe the narratives they examine as follows:

> These acts of remembering test the values that nations profess to live by against the actual experiences and perceptions of the storyteller as witness. They issue an ethical call to listeners both within and beyond national borders to recognise the disjunction between the values espoused by the community and the actual practices that occur. (2004: 3)

Both *Maus* and *The Woman Warrior* test 'American' values; specifically, in Berlant's terms, a commitment to the 'national promise' of democratic principles of freedom and equality and the mythology of the American Dream. They test those values, by considering America in relation to other nations and cultures. The Holocaust in Europe is central to Spiegelman's history, while Kingston's narrative examines the difficult assimilation of a Chinese American family. Consideration of America in this transnational (relational) sense can, therefore, be read as a call to resist the exceptionalist view of American values privileged by many autobiographies and a plea for recognition of 'other' values, other ways of representing America. The political and ethical projects of both of these autobiographies, like many of those by 'other subjects' (Anderson 2011: 86), might therefore be described as one of giving voice to the self and to others, usually members of an identity group which the writer feels him or herself to belong. No less than the 'representative men', however, these autobiographers must negotiate the difficult question of whether, and

how, they can be representative. What do these texts promise? Do they
really give voice or do they take it away? Smith and Schaeffer's figuring
of the reader as 'listener' is also striking, lending further resonance to
Hejinian's 'lobes of autobiography'. Might this imply a conception of
autobiography as something which, in an effort to make its political and
ethical points, grabs readers (not always gently) by the ears?

Maxine Hong Kingston's *The Woman Warrior* (1977) describes Kingston's experience of growing up in San Francisco, the daughter of Chinese
immigrants. As such, Kingston perceives herself to be an outsider in
America, but she also feels distanced from the Chinese cultural values
which the older generations of her family, including her parents, live
by. Kingston's text constitutes an attempt to illustrate what it is like for
an Asian-American woman negotiating relationships to two cultures,
engaging with aspects of both, but, ultimately, perhaps, belonging to
none. However, this does not prevent Kingston from being read as
'representative'. Sidonie Smith argues that the text is 'an autobiography
about women's autobiographical storytelling' (Smith, in Wong 1999: 57),
while Sau-Ling Cynthia Wong, in a discussion of the reception of the
text, outlines some of the pressures on what she calls 'the ethnic American
autobiographer', who is often considered to have certain obligations:

> to provide a positive portrayal of the ethnic community through one's
> self-portrayal. At the very least, the autobiographer's work should
> be innocent of material that might be seized upon by unsympathetic
> outsiders to illustrate prevalent stereotypes of the ethnic group; the
> author should stress the diversity of experience within the group and
> the uniqueness and self-definition of the individual. Ideally, an ethnic
> autobiography should also be a history in microcosm of the commu-
> nity, especially of its sufferings, struggles, and triumphs over racism.
> In other words, the ethnic autobiographer should be an exemplar and
> spokesman whose life will inspire the writer's own people as well as
> enlighten the ignorant about social truths. (Wong 1999: 37)

Wong cites this daunting list of interdicts not to endorse them, but in
order to make way for her own sophisticated discussion, which makes the
case for a less rigid understanding of the potential uses of autobiography,
as produced by multi-ethnic writers – Kingston, in particular. This list
of interdicts is nonetheless useful, because it sketches the many sensitive
issues likely to affect the reception of such autobiographies, related to the
burden of being 'representative', and likely to render the 'transactional'

capacity of such autobiographies perilous. In a neat reversal of Franklin's issuing of his list of virtues, in order for his readers to emulate if they should so choose, it seems that readers also have the potential to, in effect, issue their own list of maxims, which an autobiographer may feel encouraged or pressured to abide by (particularly if she or he belongs to a subordinated group), but which he or she can also refuse.

Unsurprisingly, language, speech, storytelling and writing provide the means by which Kingston registers her sense of disconnection. Many of the traumatic events Kingston recounts, which take place in her youth, pertain to the inability to speak or the perils of miscommunication. She describes how her early school years are marked by silence:

> During the first silent year I spoke to no one at school, did not ask before going to the lavatory, and flunked kindergarten. My sister also said nothing for three years, silent in the playground and silent at lunch. There were other quiet Chinese girls not of our family, but most of them got over it sooner than we did. I enjoyed the silence. At first it did not occur to me I was supposed to talk or pass kindergarten. I talked at home and to one or two of the Chinese kids in class. I made motions and even made some jokes. I drank out of a toy saucer when the water spilled out of the cup, and everybody laughed, pointing at me, so I did it some more. I didn't know that Americans don't drink out of saucers. (1977: 149)

As a child, Kingston does perceive her existence as taking the form of interdicts; she has an awareness that daily life is constituted by a series of 'dos' and 'do nots', but not knowing the precise nature of the rules in America, she continually breaks them (she doesn't talk; she drinks out of a saucer). Speech also provides the means by which she articulates her relationships, her sense of living between two cultures. If silence registers her sense of not belonging in her classroom, thus dramatising her larger cultural displacement (she mentions 'Americans'), then her admission that she talks 'at home' suggests that she is, at this stage, more comfortable with her immediate family and with Chinese culture.

In both Chinese and American cultures, however, women are accorded secondary status. Kingston is frightened and angered by the numerous ways in which she feels her Chinese relatives teach her the proverb that: "'There's no profit in raising girls. Better to raise geese than girls'" (1977: 48). At the same time, she is 'having to turn myself American-feminine, or no dates' (1977: 49). By comparing the treatment of women in both cultures and noting their oppression in both, Kingston questions the ways in which Chinese culture is perceived to be 'other' and inferior, in relation to America. The text also focuses intensely on the strained relationship between Kingston and her mother, who, like Kingston, is a storyteller, but whose stories often take the forms of cautionary tales regarding female behaviour and which Kingston struggles to interpret. *The Woman Warrior*, like *Maus*, describes a painful situation, in which a parent and child fail to understand each other's worlds and values, due to a generational estrangement caused by the pressures (the successes and failures or resistances) of assimilation. Both *The Woman Warrior* and *Maus* enlist autobiography as a means to dramatise and heal that generational rupture.

Kingston's text begins with an interdict:

> 'You must not tell anyone,' my mother said, 'what I am about to tell you. In China your father had a sister who killed herself. She jumped into the family well. We say that your father has all brothers because it is as if she had never been born.' (1977: 11)

Smith argues that this story 'concludes with forceful injunctions and powerful maxims inscribing the filial obligations of daughters in the patriarchal order' (1987: 60). Kingston's recounting of this story flouts those maxims; but her mother flouts them too, recounting the story to her daughter, rendering the moral of the tale difficult to ascertain. Kingston's mother recounts a cautionary tale – one which posits silence as ideal female behaviour and offers death as punishment for disobedience (60). The story is about Kingston's unmarried aunt, who became pregnant, under circumstances which are not made clear. As Smith notes, Kingston's mother's story is also about female disobedience and the power of female agency, because although the aunt commits suicide by jumping into the well, she poisons the family's water, exacting revenge on the family that has ostracised and punished her (62). This ensures that she will not, in fact, be forgotten (Kingston's mother continues to tell her tale). In this opening paragraph, Kingston refuses silence, refusing to observe traditional Chinese cultural dictates about the role of women. Her autobiography is an act of disobedience towards her mother, one which makes the reader complicit in the ethical dilemma it constitutes.

The Woman Warrior documents Kingston's effort to find a voice, the autobiography itself testifying to the success of that search. Storytelling, speech, silence and the power of words take the form of a complex 'inheritance' delivered to Kingston by her mother. That inheritance pertains to the ambiguous truth-status of storytelling and the responsibilities that storytelling places on a story's listener, who must determine the meaning of the story (as readers of the autobiography must also do). Towards the end of the text, Kingston admits that she continually struggles to tell when her mother is telling a story which contains true events:

> What I'll inherit someday is a green address book full of names. I'll send the relatives money, and they'll write me stories about their hunger. My mother has been tearing up the letters from the youngest grandson of her father's third wife. He has been asking for fifty dollars to buy a bicycle. He says a bicycle will change his life. He could feed his wife and children if he had a bicycle. 'We'd have to go hungry ourselves,' my mother says. 'They don't understand that we have ourselves to feed too.' I've been making money; I guess it's my turn. I'd like to go to China and see those people and find out what's a cheat story and what's not. Did my grandmother really live to be ninety-nine? Or did they string us along all those years to get our money? Do the babies wear a Mao button like a drop of blood on their jumpsuits? When we overseas Chinese send money, do the relatives divide it evenly among the commune? Or do they really pay two per cent tax and keep the rest? It would be good if the Communists were taking care of themselves; then I could buy a colour TV. (1977: 183–4)

Later, Kingston notes that her stories are 'twisted into designs' and claims that '[i]f I had lived in China, I would have been an outlaw knot-maker' (1977: 147). The ability to construct 'cruel knot[s]' (147) of stories is shared by mother and daughter, and it is not dependent on Kingston living in China. It is, in fact, part of the 'inheritance' Kingston cites, above, in an anecdote which itself constitutes one such knot. An ethics of familial obligation (what does Kingston owe her relatives in China?) and an ethics of autobiographical storytelling (in what ways can storytelling be profitable for Kingston and her relatives? Is it reprehensible to use stories in this way?) are twisted together. Structurally, too, readers might experience *The Woman Warrior* as cruelly knotted. Its five parts (lobes?) are not arranged sequentially, in any linear fashion; Kingston does not always feature prominently in them; some sections seem fictional and do not document Kingston's personal history in a sense readers might understand as literal, so that in terms of reference and genre, the text does not resemble an autobiography in any conventional sense. In its emphasis on hybridity and fragmentation, the text is clearly designed to reflect Kingston's sense of living between two cultures, and the fact that the text does not fit Lejeune's definition of autobiography is one reflection of this. And although Kingston does not mention it, surely her ability (and that of readers) to disentangle the knots is as crucial and important as her ability to make them. The text can be considered an example of a postmodern autobiography, in that it suggests that the fictions Kingston constructs, and which are handed to her by her mother, constitute truths, despite not being verifiable or provable.

With the publication of *The Woman Warrior*, though, Kingston was attacked by members of the Asian-American community for her portrayal of men. She was also attacked for her creative use of traditional Chinese tales in her work (Wong 1999: 33–4). It is certainly true that *The Woman Writer* revises traditional Chinese tales, but, again, arguably, Kingston does so explicitly, not because she is trying to distort Chinese history, but because she is engaged in thinking about how those traditional tales can be transformed in Asian-American culture. She is aware that stories are informed by, and understood differently in, different countries and different historical periods. *The Woman Warrior* is, then, a highly experimental text, which transgresses rules of genre, just as Kingston breaks the rules about what is, apparently, appropriate female behaviour for an Asian-American woman or writer.

Following her claim that she would be an 'outlaw knot-maker', Kingston speculates that '[m]aybe that's why my mother cut my tongue'. She explains:

> I used to curl up my tongue in front of the mirror and tauten my fraenum into a white line, itself as thin as a razor blade. I saw no scars in my mouth. I thought perhaps I had had two fraena, and she had cut one. I made other children open their mouths so I could compare theirs to mine. I saw perfect pink membranes stretching into precise edges that looked easy enough to cut. Sometimes I felt very proud that my mother committed such a powerful act upon me. At other times I was terrified – the first thing my mother did when she saw me was to cut my tongue.
> 'Why did you do that to me, mother?'
> 'I told you.'
> 'Tell me again.'
> 'I cut it so that you would not be tongue tied. Your tongue would be able to move in any language. You'll be able to speak languages

which are completely different from one another. You'll be able to pronounce anything. Your fraenum looked too tight to do those things, so I cut it.'
'But isn't "a ready tongue an evil"?'
'Things are different in this ghost country.' (1977: 148)

Kingston's mother's act of cutting the tongue underlines the violence and ethical costs which her daughter's acts of finding her voice are predicated upon and the pain of her complex 'inheritance'. The act of cutting the fraenum (a membrane restricting the tongue's motion) is done to give her daughter greater freedom of speech, something which will supposedly facilitate her ability to inhabit different languages and cultures. Yet, immediately after the recounting of this conversation, Kingston describes her difficulties talking, her silence in school, her embarrassment and discomfort with her own voice – something which has persisted into adulthood, despite Kingston's admission that 'I'm getting better', and 'I am making progress, a little every day' (1977: 149). Not only this, but, apparently, such violence is necessary to enable Kingston to speak *in America* – what she and her mother call the 'ghost country'. The cutting of the tongue undermines Kingston's mother's insistence that, in America, 'things are different', where Chinese maxims ('But isn't "a ready tongue an evil"?') can supposedly be disregarded. This is because although this violent act is supposed to aid Kingston, it functions as a sinister realisation of her earlier lament: 'There is a Chinese word for the female *I* – which is "slave". Break the women with their own tongues!' (1977: 49). The cutting of the tongue functions to part, to separate membrane from mouth. It is perhaps supposed to separate Kingston from her Chinese heritage, but it functions, rather, to emphasise similarities between Chinese and American culture. It signifies Kingston's position between two cultures and the difficulties of articulating that position. The passage above is notable for its doublings and hauntings – Kingston needs her mother to repeat the story of why her tongue was cut; American and Chinese cultures seem to haunt and unsettle each other; Kingston wonders if she has two fraena, rather than one. In relation to the act of cutting Kingston's tongue, Hejinian's phrase – 'the lobes of autobiography' – understood as describing autobiography as the relations between parts, now appears to promise not an affirmative reading of relationships, but one altogether more ominous than might appear within the context of *My Life*.

Victoria A. Elmwood argues that *Maus* (1996) expresses 'the author's need to write himself into a family from whose founding trauma he is absent' (Elmwood 2004: 691). *Maus* shows that a text's 'autobiographical occasion' may be an event not described in the text; it may even be an event which did not take place in the writer's lifetime. A clear indicator of the importance of relations of all sorts to *Maus*, then, is its dramatisation of the fact that an individual's life may be irrevocably affected by events which happened to others. The autobiographical occasion of *Maus* is the Holocaust, and Art's goal in the text is to determine his relationship to a history from which he feels excluded (1996: 691). Art's parents, Anja and Vladek, are Holocaust survivors. They had a son – Art's brother, Richieu – who perished during the years of the Holocaust. Art is the only family member who has not had direct experience of the Holocaust. This does not prevent the Holocaust from having an all-consuming effect on his life, not least because he feels that his lack of experience causes estrangement from his family members. His relationship with his father is strained, because of the gap in experience and understanding which separates them. Tensions between father and son are emblematised and exacerbated by their cultural estrangement; Vladek is tied to his European past, while Art was born in America. Marianne Hirsch argues that *Maus* constitutes 'the creation of postmemory' – postmemory referring to the memories that are not one's own, formed 'in relation to a familial or cultural past marked by trauma' and, therefore, usually experienced by the generation subsequent to the individuals who experienced the trauma directly (1997: 36, 127). Spiegelman's aim, in writing this autobiographical text, is to represent the legacy of the Holocaust, as made manifest in his relationship to his father. The process of constructing the text (which necessitates father and son spending a great deal of time together, the son having to listen to the father), and the final text itself, are perhaps supposed to be redemptive – some means of repairing their fractured relationship.

Vladek's identity and existence are entirely determined by the lasting traumatic effects of his experiences during the Holocaust. Many of his anxieties and behaviours (such as his refusal to let food items go to waste, his constant counting of pills) are provoked by his past experiences. Art is particularly troubled by Vladek's sense that, in comparison to the suffering invoked by the Holocaust, nothing else is valid – something which renders Art's own experiences unimportant (1996: 6). It is also suggested that he holds Vladek partially to blame for his mother's suicide (at least partly caused, it is suggested, by her inability to cope with the traumatic events in her past) – a loss which Art is dealing with throughout the text and which the autobiography may be trying to assuage. Fascinatingly, the first book, or part, of *Maus* (which was published separately in 1986) concludes with Art calling his father a 'murderer', in response to Vladek's act of destroying Anja's diaries (1996: 161). This single incident is one of the most troubling examples of the ways in which life writing can do harm and in which harm can come to life writing. Vladek's gesture is problematic. In that he decides he has the right to destroy her diaries, he claims Anja's story as his property, which may be misguided. His gesture has the obvious consequence of ensuring that her story is never heard. Art's anger about this is only compounded by the fact that one of the few lines from her writings which Vladek can recall is: '"I wish my son, when he grows up, he will be interested by this"' (1996: 161), so that Vladek may have interrupted a transaction in which Anja's autobiography should have been passed, as a gift, to her son. But Art calls Vladek a 'murderer'. For him, Anja's autobiography stands in metonymically for her (it represents her, in her absence – to destroy the diary is to destroy her). Art conflates autobiography and the author, which is also extremely problematic; especially so, perhaps, given the context of the Holocaust. This conflation of self, life and writing might also be seen in the fact that Art possibly prioritises texts over people; there is a sense that he is more interested in Vladek's past as material for an artwork, less interested in engaging with him in the present.

Elmwood suggests that 'the comics medium provides space in which both men share input in the eventual product' (2004: 691). However, this suggests that *Maus* is undertaken in a generous spirit and conceives of the autobiography as utopian space, successfully enabling the healing of the rupture between father and son. The conflict over the destruction of the diaries amply undermines both claims, and, indeed, Elmwood notes that the text does not 'make a satisfactory space for Anja' (2004: 691). One of the many profound questions explored by this text concerns the ethics of representing, and profiting from, the personal trauma of another, with specific reference to the trauma of the Holocaust. Early in the text, Art records that his father urges him not to publish what he is saying: '"such *private* things, I don't want you should mention"'. Art replies, '"Okay, okay – I promise"' (1996: 25). It is a promise Art breaks, in what Emily Miller Budick calls 'a kind of negative speech act' (2001: 379), complicated by his (honest) confession that he is breaking it. If a promise signals intent to carry out action in the future, then Art's breaking of the promise would suggest that he is, indeed, more interested in Vladek's past, more interested in the 'writing', than the 'self' or the 'life'. Miller Budick argues that '[f]rom its inception, then, the text as text constitutes a sustained act of violation: a narrative that narrates what it is forbidden to say' (2001: 379). (Not incidentally, Kingston's text can be understood as taking the form of such a 'negative speech act', too). Miller Budick questions what might make this violation justifiable and concludes that it 'does not change the success of Spiegelman's narrative that its author may still be accused at the end of having used his father's Holocaust narrative to his own psychological and artistic ends' (2001: 396). Admitting that Spiegelman's ethical stance as autobiographer may be compromised forces the reader to consider his or her own possible complicity in that betrayal, a complicity caused by the reader's decision to continue reading. This raises ethical difficulties, foregrounded by a focus on relations as central to autobiography. If identity is relational, and no individual life is lived in isolation from others, then the interconnections with those others must be represented in the autobiography. But that process of representing or documenting encounters with others may involve distortion or appropriation of details in the life of those others and may constitute a betrayal of trust or privacy (Eakin 2004: 8–9).

The relational model of identity that *Maus* relies upon raises additional questions of generic classification. The text could be read as the biography of the father, rather than, or in addition to, the autobiography of the son. Understanding *Maus* as a collaborative enterprise between father and son – one which may be mirrored in the collaboration of word and image in the graphic novel format, as Claudia Rifkind notes (2008: 402) – need not lead to the kind of tortured pondering of problems of generic classification from which Lejeune's work suffers. Rather, the many ethical dilemmas in *Maus* dramatise the difficulties of determining just how identity (and autobiography, too, perhaps) may be considered individual property. And lest this comprise an overly generous reading of the text, owing to recognition of its seemingly honest foregrounding of, and confrontation with, these difficult ethical issues, it should be noted that no matter whose story readers may believe to be foregrounded (that is, whether we think the story being told in *Maus* is Vladek's or Art's), it is, at all times, Art's version of events, and Art's artistic and ethical decisions, which are assembled on the page. As mediated by Art (*because* of the mediation), the relationship between father and son is never a relationship of equals. A relational model of identity is not necessarily a more egalitarian one.

The ethical and generic difficulties raised by *Maus* coalesce in its treatment of referentiality. Spiegelman chooses to render humans as animals, so that his text is clearly informed by post-structuralist contentions regarding the provisional and plural, the uncertain nature of truth. Jews in *Maus* are mice; Germans are cats; Poles are pigs; and Americans are dogs. However, there are moments in the text which challenge such a schematic; for example, the fact that Art is undecided about how to represent his French, Jewish wife (1996: 171) suggests that his decisions constitute only one manner of representation, in addition to raising difficult questions about whether Jewish identity signals race or ethnicity and whether either of these factors should override nationality as the criteria for representation. Ultimately, the representations present a message contradicting their simplicity; both the constructedness of identity, and the limited extent to which identities can be performed, are highlighted here. The Germans-as-cats, Jews-as-mice schematic recognises the specific historical context of the Holocaust and the anti-Semitic discourse, claiming that Jews were vermin – subhuman. Additionally, it makes the point that while individuals may be able to fashion their own identities, this is ultimately circumscribed by many factors, not least of which being the cultural and ideological contexts in which they live. *Maus* suggests that an individual's self-perception may not matter as much as others represent them (especially if an individual belongs to an oppressed identity group). The fact that Jewish identity was constructed by Nazi ideology might be considered, perhaps, in relation to the fact that, within *Maus*, the American Art determines how to represent others, especially Vladek. It is via consideration of Art's authority (authorship) that *Maus* critiques the power and global reach of America's capitalist and consumerist post-war culture; in particular, how these factors might facilitate trivialisation of the Holocaust, by turning it into commodity, spectacle, entertainment. This fact, along with the text's acknowledgement of the racism which exists in America (1996: 259–60), makes it clear that the ethical problems provoked by the Holocaust and its aftermath must be considered in relation to, and have implications for, America.

A graphic novel concerning the life of its creator (a graphic novelist), Vladek's and Art's histories are relayed via both words and images. *Maus* includes historical sources, photographs and drawings. Gillian Whitlock notes that the mixed medium of the text also poses difficult ethical questions: 'How do we do more than consume these images as passive spectators? How can we move on to recognise the norms that govern which lives will be regarded as human, and the frames through which discourse and visual representation proceed?' (2006: 965). While the text's use of photographs may ostensibly counter the danger that the use of anthropomorphic figures will fictionalise the Holocaust and Art's family history, the photographs, too, only serve to reflect one of the central problems of autobiography – that writing autobiography may distort, create or mediate the 'reality' and 'truth' it purports to capture. Sean Ross Meehan notes the fascination that 'a fundamentally metonymic condition of photography' holds for many people and cites scholarly descriptions of photographs as, variously, 'skin', 'umbilical cord' and 'footprint', as examples of such metonymic understanding (2008: 31). Such an understanding of photographs grants them the power to offer unmediated access to the real – as parts and pieces of the real, in fact. This supposedly unmediated quality offered by the metonymic quality of photographs is illustrative in understanding the close relationship between photography and autobiography in the nineteenth-century autobiographies that Meehan examines. Even more importantly, his analysis suggests that autobiography, in its pursuit of the truth, aspires to that metonymic quality of photography. Of course, this is only one way of understanding photography, and Meehan is quite aware of its problems. In her meditation on the relationship between photography and autobiography, Haverty Rugg claims:

> The insertion of photography (either as object or metaphor) into an autobiographical text can thus cut both ways. On the one hand, photographs disrupt the singularity of the autobiographical pact by pointing to a plurality of selves; not only this image but this one, this one and that one are the author. On the other hand, photographs in an autobiographical context also insist on something material, the *embodied* subject, the unification (to recall the autobiographical pact) of author, name, *and* body. (1997: 13)

This argument makes it clear that photographs may function in an autobiography to provide some guarantee of truth (these people really exist; these events really happened). In so doing, they constitute a point of reference to the world outside the text and perform the role which Lejeune claims for the author – as 'straddling' the worlds within and outwith the text (11). Conversely, photographs function to prove the impossibility of guaranteeing truth; they are partial, plural, subjectively constructed images. The contradictory and paradoxical manner in which photographs can function within autobiography echo the problems which post-structural theory raises for autobiography (see, also, Adams 2000). How to write truthfully about the self in the absence of certainty about what truth or identity entails? Depending on the autobiographer and the reader, photographs may provide the solution to this crisis, which might also be characterised as one of negotiating the relationship between the 'inside' and 'outside' of the text. Photographs provide a solution, if they are understood as guaranteeing the real, or they simply represent the crisis, because they cannot be understood as guaranteeing the real. Hirsch calls photographs 'very particular instruments of remembrance, since they are perched at the edge between memory and postmemory, and also, though differently, between memory and forgetting' (1997: 22).

The autobiographies examined in this chapter confirm Miller Budick's claim that:

> Telling stories, writing fictions, is by no means an innocent activity. In some circumstances, it may even render violence to others and to the subjects that they and we hold dear. By the end of the narrative, Vladek is tired of storytelling; it is, he tells us, enough. The same may be said of his son, who bequeaths this text, as it is, with all its perturbations and perplexities and angers and fantasies, to the reader. (2001: 396)

If constructing a fiction is not innocent, surely autobiography, with its dependence on truth, is even less innocent. While Miller Budick's use of the words 'stories' and 'fictions' to refer to *Maus* is surely problematic, it does usefully highlight the fact that for both Kingston and Spiegelman, it is in the breaking of promises and in the creating of fictions that certain truths may be found. The breaking of promises, the 'negative speech acts' central to the act of giving and finding voice in both texts, also reflect profound dissatisfaction with the 'national promise' of democracy in America – a promise with a truth-status which is also difficult to determine. Austin argues that:

> In the particular case of promising, as with so many other performatives, it is appropriate that the person uttering the promise should have a certain intention, viz. here to keep his word: and perhaps of all concomitants this looks to be the most suitable to be that which 'I promise' does describe or record. (1970: 10)

Is America's promise of democratic equality, as '[un]enumerated in the law', to use Berlant's terms (1987, 18–19), more a law than a promise, in fact? More promise than law? Is that promise being kept? Is that promise an honest one, since it may represent a future ideal, rather than a present reality? Or is it a fiction, representing a state of affairs which Kingston and Spiegelman – members of 'other' groups – do not recognise? As a means of registering ambivalence about the truth-status of that 'national promise', both *The Woman Warrior* and *Maus* refuse Lejeune's definition of autobiography. As such, their texts truthfully represent the difficulties of reading truth. Fascinatingly, for these writers, it is recourse to (tilting towards?) fiction which enables this particular truth to be represented. Kingston and Spiegelman emphasise the importance of fictions in a world in which promises of equality may be fictive. In so doing, both texts register some of the uncertainties which are a feature of post-structuralist thought, but also reveal an (ethical) commitment to a verifiable truth, which might reflect wariness about those uncertainties. Paradoxically, that commitment is registered via compromising acts – violence, the breaking of promises. Kingston's text ends with the declaration that a Chinese song passed down to descendants has 'translated well' (1977: 186). *Maus* ends with Spiegelman's signature (which looks like the unravelling of one of Kingston's 'cruel knots') beneath drawings of his parents' tombstones. In both cases, it is unclear whether the autobiographer has finally managed to, or desires to, reconcile (or be reconciled to) 'the lobes of autobiography'.

CHAPTER 4

Gender, Illness and Autobiography

As I look ahead, I feel like a man who has awakened from a long afternoon nap to find the evening stretched out before me. I'm reminded
of D'Annunzio, the Italian poet, who said to a duchess he had just met
at a party in Paris, 'Come, we will have a profound evening.' Why
not? I see the balance of my life – everything comes in images now –
as a beautiful paisley shawl thrown over a grand piano.

Why a paisley shawl, precisely? Why a grand piano? I have no
idea. That's how the situation presents itself to me. I have to take my
imagery along with my medicine. (Broyard 1992: 7)

For Anatole Broyard, as for so many others, the experience of suffering
illness (in Broyard's case, prostate cancer) constitutes an important
autobiographical occasion – the opportunity to reflect on his life. Writers
have always written autobiographically about illness, and autobiographies of illness seem to consistently engage readers' interest, but,
currently, autobiographies of illness receive significant critical attention.
This chapter opens by suggesting why this might be the case. It will then
consider the relationship of gender and genre in two autobiographies –
Lucy Grealy's *Autobiography of a Face* (1994) and Lance Armstrong's *It's
Not About the Bike* (2001). This chapter also revisits many of the themes
and problems identified in previous chapters, as central to the study of
autobiography.

Broyard indirectly, but clearly, encourages readers to join him in
his search to make meaning out of his illness: 'Why a paisley shawl,
precisely? Why a grand piano? I have no idea'. Broyard's claim that he
does not have the answers, and his fascination with his own imagery –
which he describes as taking the form of a gift, delivered in parts (succes-
sive images present themselves) – suggests that, for him, the author is
not a privileged site of authority and that meaning is generated by the
relations between signs and between autobiographer and reader. His

autobiography, *Intoxicated By My Illness* (1992), can be understood as reflecting a version of identity as relational, as discussed in the previous chapter. His discussion also takes the form of a meditation on the politics (and erotics) of identification. Broyard attempts to communicate his sense of being 'intoxicated by his illness', via the trope of seduction, ostensibly structured by heterosexual desire. However, the rejoinder 'Why not?' suggests that Broyard identifies with the duchess, who is possibly being seduced by the male poet; it is her position which he imaginatively occupies. Broyard's illness is represented as causing what could be called a 'queering' of identity and relationships. Eve Sedgwick defines the word 'queer' as follows:

> Queer is a continuing moment, movement, motive – recurrent, eddying, *troublant*. The word 'queer' itself means *across* – it comes from the Indo-European root – *twerkw*, which also yields the German *quer* (transverse), Latin *torquere* (to twist), English *athwart*. [...] The immemorial current that *queer* represents is antiseparatist [sic] as it is antiassimilationist [sic]. Keenly, it is relational, and strange. (1994: viii)

In that Broyard figures his identity (when sick, as a vulnerable, passive patient) as 'feminine', for him, illness entails loss of masculinity, suggesting that he subscribes to essentialist categories of gender (there is evidence for this in the text). But his point may be more radical. He may be suggesting that illness exposes the cultural constructions of masculinity and femininity to be *only* constructions. As such, the experience of illness prompts a sense of identity as strange, relational; prompting the sense of joy and wonder in self-discovery, which Broyard's text often exhibits.

Broyard's speculations encapsulate the central claims made in this chapter. Firstly, it is useful to think of autobiographies (especially those focusing on illness) as engaging in multiple, complex 'recoveries' (Broyard's imagery of the paisley shawl covering the grand piano requires acts of interpretive 'recovery', on both his part and that of the reader). Secondly, his meditation above usefully illustrates one of the final claims made in this textbook. It is hypothesised that what *might* make American autobiographies distinctively American, giving them their political and ethical impetus, is not (or not only) their acts of affirmation, as might be suspected, given their frequent aims of making various identity groups visible, giving them voice, arguing for inclusivity. Rather, what makes these texts distinctively American may be the ways in which these texts engage in acts of *refusal*. Many of the autobiographies discussed in this textbook constitute what Emily Miller Budick calls, in her reading of *Maus* (discussed in the previous chapter), 'a sort of negative speech act' – a gesture of refusal, aspiring to a performative utterance (2001: 379). Broyard's seeming acceptance of his situation ('I have to take my imagery along with my medicine') is not what it appears. His imagery of the paisley shawl and grand piano could be read as unhelpfully enigmatic. They do not necessarily constitute the gift of an illuminating image, but rather, may signal a refusal to enlighten readers. Subsequent to Broyard's death in 1990, controversy arose regarding his racial identity, stemming from the discovery that he had supposedly been 'passing' as white for much of his life. This led to speculation (and often disapproval) about the motives he may have had for doing so (see, for example, Henry Louis Gates' (1997) essay, 'The passing of Anatole Broyard'). The shawl covering (hiding?) the grand piano suggests that, for Broyard, self-representation is a creative endeavour. Autobiography involves the production of an aesthetic object (the self, the text), which both reveals and conceals, which can preserve and destroy (disturbingly, the shawl is reminiscent of a shroud).

Before accounting for the preoccupation with illness in the practice and criticism of contemporary American autobiography, it must be noted that autobiography itself has received increased critical attention over the past four decades. The reason for this is partly explained by the developments in post-structuralist theory, which had an impact on the theory and conception of autobiography from around 1970, as discussed in the previous chapter. But this is not the full story. Leigh Gilmore offers four reasons for what is often described as the 'memoir boom' of the 1990s and millennial American culture. A great many bestselling autobiographies, such as Elizabeth Wurtzel's *Prozac Nation* (1994), Mary Karr's *The Liar's Club* (1995), Frank McCourt's *Angela's Ashes* (1996) and Augusten Burroughs's *Running with Scissors* (2002), were published during this period (this is a tiny, random selection of texts). Firstly, Gilmore understands this 'memoir boom' as reflecting widespread concern in American culture with personhood and the political, with citizenship, nation and belonging. She argues that:

> the current boom in memoir would be inconceivable were it not for the social and political movements of the past thirty years that have made it possible for a broader range of people to publish accounts of

their life experiences. Women, people of color, gay men and lesbians, the disabled, and survivors of violence have contributed to the expansion of self-representation by illuminating suppressed histories and creating new emphases. (2001: 16)

While not incorrect, Gilmore overstates the 'new' here. Consideration of the texts discussed in the first two chapters of this textbook reveals that autobiography has *always* reflected concerns with personhood, citizenship, nation and belonging, and it has *always* been written by this 'broader range of people'; the real difference, in recent decades, concerns the quantity of texts being published and the increasing receptiveness towards autobiographies written by individuals belonging to the groups Gilmore cites. Secondly, Gilmore explains that 'the media confessional, and also "real life" media that posit a naturalised speaker who is simply telling his or her story, have come to permeate contemporary American culture', adding that this confessional media climate only supplements and does not displace the pre-existing popularity of print autobiographies (2001: 17). Thirdly, in recent decades, the autobiographical 'I' appeared in new venues; Gilmore cites personal criticism and creative nonfiction as examples (Broyard's autobiographical essays about his illness have affiliations with both). Finally, she points to the fact that the literary market has increasingly encouraged autobiographical writing, reflecting the perception that 'it sells to tell your story' (2001: 17). The 'media confessional' climate Gilmore describes has only intensified, and the new venues for the autobiographical 'I' only proliferated in the twenty-first century, with the use of digital media and social networking sites and activities, such as Twitter, Facebook, YouTube and blogging, which intensify that sense that every individual has a story to tell, any individual can be exceptional (the ways in which these sites and activities may extend and revise the possibilities of autobiography – in particular, with regard to reference, truth, relational identity and relations to readers, are beginning to be realised and assessed, and marks one significant direction in which the study of autobiography is likely to develop in the future: for example, in the burgeoning criticism on autobiography and the posthuman[1]). Yet, paradoxically, it may be difficult to be exceptional in the late twentieth and twenty-first centuries, more difficult to get one's voice heard. It might be for these reasons that many of the bestselling autobiographies of the 'memoir boom', including those cited above, focus on deeply unhappy experiences of physical and mental health problems, unhappy childhoods. The 1990s 'memoir boom' has also been understood as a boom in the 'misery memoir' (Anderson 2011: 115–16). Many critical studies of autobiography during this period reflect an emphasis on the representation of trauma (see, for example, Ashley et al. (1994), Henke (2000) and Rogers et al. (2004)). That focus on trauma is both a contributory factor in producing the confessional culture Gilmore cites and a product of that culture; trauma is a major focus in Gilmore's own work.

The factors Gilmore cites go a considerable way towards providing context and explanation for the appeal of illness as a subject for writers and readers of autobiography. The sick or disabled subject is one whose experiences have become more visible in the last three or four decades; so much so, in fact, that G. Thomas Couser argues that: 'the much bally-hooed "memoir boom" has also been a boom in disability life writing, although publishers and reviewers rarely, if ever, acknowledge it as such' (2009: 2). A rare or painful illness could render an individual exceptional, yet illness is a common human experience with which readers can sympathise (the autobiographer can be both unique and representative). For example, Arthur W. Frank introduces his study of narratives of illness by arguing that: 'the ill person who turns illness into story transforms fate into experience; the disease that sets the body apart from others becomes, in the story, the common bond of suffering that joins bodies in their shared vulnerability' (1995: xi). Anne Hunsaker Hawkins notes that: 'it is striking that autobiographical descriptions of illness should belong almost exclusively to the second part of the twentieth century' (1999: 11). She suggests that, whereas in previous centuries, illness was accepted as part of the process of living and dying, techno-logical and medical developments have contributed to a late twentieth century construction of illness as aberrant, something to be marked off from 'normal life' (1999: 11). She explains that autobiographies of illness 'are compelling because they describe dramatic human experience of real crisis: they appeal to us because they give shape to our deepest hopes and fears about such crises, and in so doing, they often draw upon profound archetypal dimensions of human experience' (1999: 31).

An autobiography of illness testifies to a simple, but momentous fact: the writer has survived to tell the tale. An autobiography of illness might reveal a desire present in *all* autobiography; testifying to one's existence is simultaneously to forestall death. As Gilmore says:

An autobiography is a monument to the idea of personhood, to the notion that one could leave behind a memorial to oneself (just in case

no one else ever gets around to it) and that the memorial would perform
the work of permanence that the person never can. (2001: 12–13)

The autobiography here functions ambiguously – it either metonymically stands in for (replaces) the author in his or her absence, in effect,
cancelling out that absence, or it leaves a trace of the author. Hawkins
argues for the centrality of myth in autobiographies of illness (1999:
18), noting that, for example, autobiographies of illness often invoke
the myth of the personal journey (1999: 19), thus providing the opportunity for self-examination. Writers may use the experience of illness as
a catalyst for re-evaluation of their behaviour and values. This examination may or may not have spiritual significance, but, nonetheless,
reveals that autobiographies of illness provide the occasion for narratives of restoration, transformation and recovery: certainly, many illness
autobiographies share features of spiritual autobiography. Writers ask,
and explain, how their experience of illness has changed their sense of
who they are. Perhaps illness has affected an individual's physical appearance (as it does in the case of Lucy Grealy). Perhaps it has prevented an
individual from carrying out the professional or personal roles which
previously defined him or her (as with Lance Armstrong). From the
retrospective position of recovery, the writer feels that he or she has a
changed worldview or list of priorities, so that autobiographies of illness
often constitute what Hawkins calls 'rebirth narratives' (1999: 31).

Many autobiographies of illness describe an uplifting, inspiring
narrative of heroically beating the odds; something which, within an
American cultural context, could allow for a celebration of individualism. Autobiographies of illness allow the possibility of a profound
meditation on the nature of luck, fate and survival (why me?). American
autobiographies exploring these themes may be more likely to critique
that ideology of individualism. Hawkins also suggests that the emergence
of illness as an important subject for autobiography in the late twentieth
century may be explained by a desire to counter the de-personalisation
and voicelessness which individuals often experience in their new identities as patients (1999: 11), so that these autobiographies enable the writer
to protest on behalf of those suffering from a particular illness. Writers
petition for changes in the law, amendments to healthcare provision,
more scientific research in pursuit of a cure. A writer may wish to protest
against prejudice and discrimination and, thus, encourage a readership to
think differently about the sick or disabled. He or she may offer advice to
readers suffering from the same illness, offering practical tips regarding

cures, consolatory support or generalised life lessons in the mode of the self-help narrative. The desire for such advice may constitute the central reason why readers read autobiographies about illness. Readers may have a voyeuristic curiosity about the symptoms and sufferings of others. They may wish to know what being ill is like. They may engage, in Nancy Miller's terms, in complex acts of (dis?) identification with the suffering subject (2002: xv–vi).

Autobiographies of illness also necessarily foreground the body. As such, and like some of the autobiographies discussed in this study, they refuse to accept the traditional privileging of 'mind' over body in Western culture. This is another way in which autobiography in Western cultures may challenge (refuse?) the very Enlightenment ideologies which nonetheless produce it. Linda Haverty Rugg argues, in fact, that the body is one of the primary touchstones of reference in autobiography (1997: 20). It is the body of the autobiographer which she primarily has in mind, but, surely, her point can extend to the reader's body, too. She insists on the referential importance of the body, because this can challenge or correct post-structuralist and postmodern conceptions of 'truth' or 'the real' as somehow non-existent or, because impossible to define, not worthy of serious examination: 'the trick is seeing both the material body and its constructed nature at the same time' (1997: 20). Autobiographies of illness, then, have an important part to play in discussions about truth and reference. Indeed, autobiographies of illness may, as Gilmore suggests in her recent work, be considered an occasion for considering the relationship between autobiography and the posthuman (Gilmore 2012).

Many of the reasons for writing autobiographies of illness cited above can be understood as constituting various kinds of attempted 'recoveries' – a trope useful not only for autobiographies of illness, but for autobiography generally. One example provides an illustration of these complex senses of autobiography as recovery. In her autobiography, *A Good Enough Daughter* (1999), focusing on the illness and death of her parents, Alix Kates Shulman describes 'the paradox of memory that had troubled me since I began to write' (1999: 71):

> I think of my memory as the secret storeroom at the heart of a maze; there's only one key, and I have it. Behind the door my memories rest like dormant seeds full of potential second life that can't begin till I shine light on them. Like the record of the past preserved in lava and ice, in wrecks and ruins, my memories are safe there – for the time

being. But like buried treasure that turns to dust when it hits the air, once memories are delivered from private custody to the world, they become endangered. Touch them back to life, and like everything alive they begin the inescapable process of corruption, confusion, decay, the end of which is rigor mortis. As Italo Calvino succinctly put it, memory 'is true only as long as you do not set it, as long as it is not enclosed in a form.' While they remain private and unanalysed, memories have all the magic and power of imagination itself. But once you seize and pin them down, once you snap the picture or write the book, they lose their shimmering complexity, their rich associations, their romance and ambiguity until, diminished and degraded, they are lost as surely as if synapses had been destroyed, and you can no longer diminish what's true from what's been depicted. The work, having fattened on memory, may acquire a life of its own, but the memories lie on the ground inert, like desiccated husks. This is why after I've plundered my memories for a story I can no longer tell what really took place – as prisoners forced to spill their secrets are said to lose their power to know the truth. (1999: 71)

Autobiography might be understood as a project of recovery – a means of delivering memories 'from private custody to the world' (this figures the autobiographer as caretaker, custodian, messenger bearing gifts) (1999: 71). Nicola King argues that '[c]onsistency of consciousness and a sense of continuity between the actions and events of the past, and the experience of the present, would appear to be integral to a sense of personal identity' (2000: 2), so that memory is key to construction of the self and the past presented in autobiography. Of course, such projects of recovery are far from simple (what are the implications for identity and autobiography for those of us – all of us – who cannot remember parts of their lives due to ageing or trauma, for example?). King draws attention to two ways of conceiving memory, both of which are apparent in Shulman's passage, above:

One model, illustrated by Freud by means of an analogy with archaeological excavation, assumes that the past still exists 'somewhere', waiting to be rediscovered by the remembering subject, uncontaminated by subsequent experience and time's attrition. The other imagines the process of memory as one of continuous revision or 'retranslation', reworking memory-traces in the light of later knowledge and experience. (2000: 4)

In Shulman's analysis, both models of memory described by King operate simultaneously and overlap, as they do in many autobiographies. Shulman's notion of memory as a storeroom corresponds to the model of memory as excavation and would suggest that autobiography is a supposedly straightforward project of recovering the past. However, Shulman ambiguously locates her memories; they are both part of her (that is, internal), but also figured as external or inaccessible to the self. Her anxieties about the ways in which recording and examining memories may alter them acknowledges that model of revision or retranslation, something she understands largely (probably too simplistically) in terms of loss and diminishment. Her discussion is simplistic, because it implies that as long as they are unexamined and untouched, memories exist in some truthful, authentic state. Yet memory is imperfect, necessitating 'retranslation', as Shulman makes clear. Any autobiographer is inevitably involved in acts of re-covering, distorting, concealing or embellishing the truth (if 'truth' even exists).

The dependence of autobiography on memory (its projects of recovery) is figured by Shulman as both healthy and unhealthy. The autobiographer is like a healer who touches memories back to life, but creating autobiography destroys memories, in a manner analogous to the progression of a disease (those destroyed synapses). Memory nurtures autobiography, providing it with sustenance (the work 'fattens on memory'), but autobiography may destroy memory, here figured as (once) living ('desiccated husks'). In that case, the autobiographer is left disoriented, the project of recovery having failed – 'after I've plundered my memories for a story I can no longer tell what really took place'.

Autobiographies of illness are narratives of recovered health, however tentative or incomplete (telling the tale proves survival). They constitute narratives of recovery, in the sense that an autobiographer often tells the story of an identity which has been recovered or 'restored'. Restoration might refer to the fact that the autobiographer's sense of self has been reconstituted as the result of a return to health and/or it might refer to the fact that illness has been a life-changing experience, prompting the autobiographer to reclaim a sense of his or her identity, who he or she 'really' is. 'Recovery' also describes the political agenda of many autobiographies of illness – that of giving voice to identities and experiences previously ignored or silenced. Finally, the trope of recovery is useful in considering the perplexities of genre classification which autobiography poses. Derrida argues that:

a text cannot belong to no genre, it cannot be without or less a genre. Every text participates in one or several genres, there is no genreless text; there is always a genre and genres, yet such participation never amounts to belonging. And not because of an abundant overflowing or a free, anarchic and unclassifiable productivity, but because of the *trait* of participation itself, because of the effect of the code and of the generic mark. (1980: 212)

A novel often contains some marker (usually in its frontispiece or copyright material) informing readers that it is a work of fiction, a novel. This information functions as a generic mark. But the mark does not belong to the novel; it is not part of the text it labels. So the mark participates, without belonging, in the genre it describes. The generic mark works – like all boundary markers – to include and exclude. To be a novel, a text must *not* be other things (poetry, non-fiction). The act of classifying genre depends on a law of non-contamination: 'Thus, as soon as genre announces itself, one must respect a norm, one must not cross a line of demarcation, one must not risk impurity, anomaly or monstrosity' (Derrida 1980: 203–4). And yet, as Derrida notes, this line of demarcation has been broken, impurity is always already incorporated in the very act of announcing the genre, via a mark which does not partake of the genre of the text. This might explain the emphasis on failure in many autobiographies. It is worth recalling Thoreau's couplet: 'My life has been the poem I would have writ / But I could not both live and utter it'. In light of Derrida's reading, autobiography might be considered an 'unhealthy' genre, because it so clearly engages with anomaly and monstrosity (an interdisciplinary genre, it does not 'belong' to a single discipline, such as fiction or history). However, what Derrida's reading suggests is that *all* texts are monstrous, unhealthy, impure, because of the 'trait of participation'. That is, autobiography reveals any notion of a 'pure' genre (figured by Derrida as a healthy one) as a fiction. The anxieties which often attend efforts to describe autobiography may be symptomatic of autobiography's (honest?) representation of its own failure, which also speaks to a condition which affects all texts or genres, but which is perhaps less often acknowledged within them. 'Health' and 'unhealth' become – in terms of this reading – difficult to determine, because Derrida has made it clear how difficult it is to distinguish between categories.

For Lucy Grealy and Lance Armstrong, cancer challenges gendered identity, troubling their sense of belonging to categories they construct as 'masculine' and 'feminine'. Armstrong suffers from testicular cancer. This threatens his strength and virility – qualities central to Armstrong's 'vision of masculinity'; as a result, his autobiography can be understood as an exercise in 'testing and proving one's manhood', which Michael Kimmel claims to be 'one of the defining experiences in American men's lives' (2006: 1–2). Grealy suffers from cancer of the jaw, resulting in facial disfigurement. She perceives herself as 'ugly' and becomes obsessed with beauty as a mark of female identity and worth. For both, illness necessitates painful questioning about identity and values, although each writer comes to very different conclusions.

While Armstrong's is the autobiography of a celebrity, Grealy's is not. Couser approvingly cites an article by Lorraine Adams, which distinguishes between two types of autobiography – the 'somebody memoir' and the 'nobody memoir' (Adams, in Couser 2009: 1). The 'somebody' memoir is written by someone known to the reading public, prior to the book's publication; the 'nobody' memoir is written by an individual who only becomes known as a result of publication. Couser finds that Adams' terminology (somebody, nobody) functions both 'usefully and insidiously' to describe autobiographies of disability (2009: 1). He attempts to refine Adams' terminology:

> I wish to point out that, ironically but significantly, the new nobody memoir is also often the memoir of *some body*. Far more than the somebody memoir, the nobody memoir is often about what it's like to have or to *be*, to live in or *as*, a particular body – indeed, a body that is usually odd or anomalous. (2009: 2)

Couser's analysis is marked by his own agenda of scholarly recovery. He wishes to account for the increasing importance and visibility of life writing on the subject of disability. His point is valid – autobiographies by lesser-known individuals often come to prominence because they are about the experience of living with illness and disability. But he exaggerates the difference between somebody and nobody memoirs. Lance Armstrong's text is a somebody memoir and, quite clearly, a some body memoir. The autobiography of a celebrity, Armstong's text is influenced by, and reflects, the demands of a popular reading audience. His status has direct consequences for the manner in which he describes his experience of illness and may determine the possible motives he claims to have in writing his autobiography. His autobiography is written with the assistance of a professional writer – the title page cites Armstrong as author, 'with Sally Jenkins'. As James W. Pipkin notes, this situation is far from unusual in autobiographies by sports celebrities:

> The most common phrases used on the title pages to describe the relationship between the athlete and the professional writer – 'as told to,' 'with,' and 'and' – are not definitive, and the same phrase may not even mean the same thing to the different athletes and collaborators who use it. If we rely on the information that is sometimes provided in the preface or the foreword to the books, what seems most clear is that the professional writer is not usually a 'ghost writer' who uses newspaper stories and magazine articles to create the story with little or no assistance from the athlete. The most common practice is for the professional writer to tape a series of interviews with the athlete, to write the chapters based upon the tapes, and then to submit the manuscript to the athlete for his or her input. This general process leaves a great deal of flexibility for what actually happens in a particular case. (2008: 9)

Dependence on a professional writer's assistance means that the degree to which Armstrong constructs or owns his text is unclear. The joint signature, the fact that Armstrong's life is presumably shaped by an individual who has not experienced either Armstrong's athletic success or the sufferings he endures as a result of his illness, constitute only two ways in which understanding his text as autobiography is problematic. Or is it? If a reader grants that identity is discovered in relation to others, might not the assistance of a professional writer simply be one illustration of this and a reminder that those relationships may not be of equals? While this situation poses significant interpretive difficulties for a reader of Armstrong's text, Grealy's autobiography is even more complex and troubling, because it refuses to offer simple or optimistic readings of her experiences. It is because of the more complex nature of Grealy's text that Armstrong's will be discussed first, although her text was published earlier.

The title of Armstrong's autobiography, *It's Not About the Bike*, is more fitting than perhaps its author intended. Ostensibly, the reference to the bike alludes to Armstrong's identity as champion athlete, twice winner of the Tour de France. However, the title urges readers to appreciate that 'it' (Armstrong's life? His autobiography? His interpretation of his life? The thing he values most in life?) is his illness, not his sporting achievements. The title constitutes the autobiography's message: it's not about the bike. Armstrong's illness prompts him to reassess what is important in his life. But in that case, just what this autobiography *is* 'about' is unclear. After all, Armstrong's sporting achievements and public persona stimulates readers' interest in his illness. His autobiography relies upon the power of what Margot Strickland calls the 'big name' (1995: 67) in selling 'some body' autobiographies. That a significant part of the autobiography charts the history of Armstrong's career would seem to suggest awareness of this expectation.

The evasive title suggests that Armstrong is conflicted about the subject of his autobiography, the lessons he and others are to gain from his experiences. His uncertainty regarding what, in fact, his book is about is made clear within the autobiography's opening pages, revealing anxiety surrounding issues of agency, ownership and responsibility. Armstrong's anxiety about what his autobiography is 'about' can be understood in relation to Derrida's reading of genre. Armstrong is not sure which genres he wishes his story to participate in. His text opens by announcing a refusal to participate in (be contaminated by?) certain genres, such as the fairy-tale or Franklinian success story (2001: 2–3). This refusal, like the claim 'it's not about the bike' and like Derrida's 'generic mark', undermines itself through the simple act of its inscription. Armstrong prepares the reader to have expectations overturned (he will speak unpleasant truths; this is no fairy-tale). But his narrative strains to be read exactly in the way he disdains – as a triumphalist fairy-tale, with Armstrong constructed as a 'Great American' (2001: 3), a representative, Franklinian role model, who converts his experience into useful lessons for others.

Two tensions animate the autobiography – and threaten to derail it. Firstly, Armstrong is uncertain about how to interpret his experience of cancer or, more specifically, his recovery. While his survival is labelled 'more a matter of blind luck' (2001: 3), the text strongly suggests that he is to be credited for having survived. Armstrong's survival is, it is suggested, at least partly due to his competitive nature, his determination to succeed, his industriousness, his powers of endurance. Central to the text is Armstrong's use of the experience of race and competition as a metaphor for the experience of suffering and eventually overcoming cancer. He claims that his doctor suggests that 'cancer is the Tour de France of illnesses' (2001: 274). From a practical perspective, that analogy makes it possible for Armstrong to describe his sporting career in great detail in the text. The problematic implications of this particular metaphor are many, and indications are that it is more than a metaphor. Armstrong claims that: '[t]he more I thought about it, the more cancer seemed like a race to me' (2001: 89). Reliance on the metaphor of cancer as race threatens to obscure the fact that this is an autobiography 'about' cancer. Is it not, in fact, all about the bike, despite Armstrong's protestations?

Armstrong's tone and writing style contribute to the text's contradictions – his assertion that he is not here to 'make polite conversation' is belied by his euphemistic allusion to 'matters below the waist' (2001: 3). Despite a desire to communicate simple, unpalatable truths, Armstrong is not clear what the truth is. If he cannot explain why he has survived, how can he present himself as a model 'fit to be imitated'? This is complicated by the fact that when it comes to his gendered identity, there *are* clear lessons he wishes to convey. For example, Armstrong uses the expectation of truth in autobiography to recount and refute, in great detail, accusations about drug tests (2001: 250–5).

Armstrong desires to claim responsibility for his survival, because he is aware of the expectations of readers who perceive him as a role model (as 'Great American') and because claiming responsibility for his survival might further 'prove' his masculine identity – an identity threatened by his particular cancer and by the passivity and weakness which threaten to define him as a cancer patient. Armstrong's account, above, of what readers can expect from his autobiography is preceded by an assertion of his gendered identity:

> A slow death is not for me. I don't do anything slow, not even breathe. I do everything at a fast cadence: eat fast, sleep fast. It makes me crazy when my wife, Kristin, drives our car, because she brakes at all the yellow caution lights, while I squirm impatiently in the passenger seat.
>
> 'Come on, don't be a skirt,' I tell her.
>
> 'Lance,' she says, 'Marry a man'. (2001: 1–2)

The present tense of this opening passage is important. Armstrong is describing his identity *post*-cancer. Despite his claim that '[t]here are two Lance Armstrongs, pre-cancer, and post' (2001: 4), the bravado, competitiveness and aggression asserted in these passages are strongly reminiscent of Armstrong's discussions of his brash, confident, younger (pre-cancer) self. Armstrong's impatience, willingness to defy authority and reluctance to be anywhere other than in the driving seat are contrasted with the behaviour of his wife, who is presented as hesitant, law-abiding.

Femininity and implied homosexuality are used as terms of insult by Armstrong and his wife. Masculinity is valorised – his scars, like his autobiography, are to be shown off as proof of it. Armstrong continually demonstrates his masculine credentials, anxious that he may not be meeting his own tough standards. The passages above are marked by reliance on binary oppositions – male/female, fast/slow, stop/go – further indicating that Armstrong prefers simple explanations and clearly defined (hierarchical) identity categories, but these are denied him by his experience of cancer (and also, perhaps, denied by his wife: 'Marry a man').

Armstrong's desire to be read within the terms of his own understanding of 'masculinity' also undermines a tentative claim he makes later in the text, offered in the manner of a Franklin-like maxim: 'If there is a defining characteristic of a man as opposed to a boy, maybe it's patience' (2001: 67). His opening passage suggests that masculinity is signalled by the absence of patience. To the extent that Armstrong's pre- and post-cancer selves are both marked by impatience, this collapses the distance between them and renders problematic his claim that he has learned valuable lessons from his cancer. It casts doubt on his declaration that: 'Cancer would change everything for me, I realised; it wouldn't just derail my career, it would deprive me of my entire definition of who I was' (2001: 14). Armstrong attempts to counter and address this threat of derailment in his text, specifically, by re-asserting his status as 'man'. In fact, Armstrong's desire is to show that, in certain vital respects, cancer has *not* changed him. His autobiography is an exercise in self-recovery, rather than self-transformation. The latter sections of the text prioritise the documentation of Armstrong's personal triumphs, post-recovery: his marriage and the birth of his son are presented as further 'proofs'; Armstrong describes how his son 'screamed like a world-class, champion screamer' (2001: 270). The text also contains a section of photographs which recapitulate the narrative of recovery told in the autobiography – these do not add new information, but seem included for the purpose of emphasising (should more emphasis be needed) that he is an exemplary American. (Viewing the narrative presented by these photos is also poignant, given the eventual breakdown of Armstrong's marriage, subsequent to the publication of this autobiography. If the reader has this knowledge, then it is more difficult, perhaps, to read Armstrong as exemplary).[2]

As noted, it is suggested that the skills enabling Armstrong to be a superlative athlete assist him in surviving cancer. But Armstrong is aware that this comes close to arguing that if an individual does not survive his or her illness, this is the fault of the individual – he or she did not try hard enough, did not possess the necessary skills of endurance and determination. However, if Armstrong abdicates responsibility for his survival, then luck is the only thing that determined his fate, meaning that he has no lessons to give, he can only document that luck. Being merely lucky robs Armstrong of the self-determination precious to him and renders him no longer an agent in his life story, affiliating him more closely with the identities of 'patient' or 'cancer victim' which he detests. As a means of avoiding these problems, Armstrong invokes that gesture of installing himself as a representative man (emphasis on 'man'), predicated upon the public association of himself with cancer:

> I am very firm in my belief that cancer is not a form of death. I choose to redefine it: it is a part of life. One afternoon when I was in remission and sitting around and waiting to find out if the cancer would come back, I made an acronym out of the word: Courage, Attitude, Never give up, Curability, Enlightenment, and Remembrance of my fellow patients. (2001: 273–4)

It is by splitting cancer (the word, the experience) into parts, and then implying that he represents (embodies) the experience in its totality, that Armstrong installs himself as representative. The acronym exercise enacts (metonymically?) Armstrong's aims in his autobiography. He desires to describe his life and its lessons as a totality of simple, clear (and clearly delineated) lessons and parts, but fails to do so. If he is merely lucky, how can he claim the agency stressed here? Another lesson comes in the form of his claim that: 'We have two options, medically and emotionally: give up, or fight like hell' (2001: 273). His combative approach to fighting cancer is characteristic of him, but it involves cliché and utilises a problematic model – dealing with illness (successfully) necessitates engaging in war – with which many feminist scholars have taken issue (see, for example, Stacey 1997; Potts 2000). However, Armstrong also stresses more abstract lessons: the value of 'hope', that 'anything is possible' (273), underscoring the precariousness of his representative role. Ultimately, his claim that 'It's not about the bike' constitutes a gesture of refusal, which, in failing so spectacularly, comes close to rendering the autobiography an untruth.

If Armstrong presents himself (despite himself) as emblematic of the attainment of the American Dream, Grealy critiques the cultural conditions which she believes make attainment of that dream impossible. Her sense of disappointment with America predates her cancer. Describing her family's move to America from Ireland, when Grealy and her twin sister, Sarah, were four, Grealy explains how the family travelled by boat, seemingly on her father's whim. Initially, the gesture signals desire to assent to American values, but, in retrospect, it refuses to be read in this way:

> Unlike our earlier countrymen, who came in steerage, we sailed on the *Queen Mary*, on what was her penultimate voyage. Surely this grand act was to be the harbinger of the riches already awaiting us. As with most of my father's gestures, that voyage was well meant, but later, when things were not going quite as well, it was referred to with scorn, and even later, after his early death, it seemed an act filled with literary bathos, and pointedly sad. (1994: 32)

One of the signs that 'things were not going quite as well' is the discovery of Grealy's cancer, made when she was nine years old. Like Armstrong, she refuses to provide an optimistic meditation about survival, but whereas Armstrong might be understood as reneging on the promise implicit in that refusal, Grealy keeps her word. Her recovery is neither joyful nor triumphalist; for example, Grealy does not provide a reading of her illness as yielding 'riches' of any sort. She explains how her older brothers are bitter about the move to America and that 'when we first arrived, I could not even eat an American candy bar without being reminded by one of my brothers that it stood for the entire political and social inferiority of America' (1994: 33). This questioning, if not hostile, relationship to American culture partially explains her refusal to embrace myths of national identity which are meaningful for Armstrong (indeed, it seems implicit that her cancer somehow mocks any understanding of America as a land of promise). This refusal is also explained by the fact that Grealy explores the traumatic effects of surgery, which left her with a facial disfigurement, destroying her sense of self-worth. In particular, Grealy critiques society's equation of female worth with beauty and the economies of commodification and desire, which she believes construct her as valueless and which are responsible for her life-long sense of stigmatisation, her frustrated search for personal happiness and the innumerable cruelties she experiences at the hands of others (1994: 124–5, 150–2). Sylvia Brown argues that Grealy's autobiography can be understood as:

implicitly addressing the following question: how can she (how can anyone?) recoup a sense of wholeness or satisfy a craving for a sense of wholeness when not merely the body's limitations but a kind of social disease reinforces feelings of incompleteness – when, as she observes, 'society tells us again and again that we can most be ourselves by looking like someone else?' (2006: 297)

Susannah B. Mintz calls Grealy's text 'an autobiography without resolution' (2007: 68). This failure to provide resolution, understood here as that sense of wholeness, might account for its relative obscurity (it has been critically praised, but receives little scholarly attention). If there is any optimism to be found here (and there might be very little, if the reader has knowledge of Grealy's death in 2002), it might be that Grealy's status as a 'no body', in Couser's terms (a term especially poignant, given Grealy's negative evaluations of herself), grants her a certain freedom to stray from the conventional plots and lessons of illness autobiographies. That is, her narrative is not circumscribed by the pressures and limitations which dictate Armstrong's narrative.

Brown argues that:

[Grealy] would write her way to wholeness and to a more stable and acceptable sense of identity amidst a fluctuating physical appearance and dominant cultural constructions of her as an object or as an incomplete person. Autobiography would seem to be the perfect genre for accomplishing her personal goals as well as the larger political agenda of disability studies and criticism. (2006: 298)

Yet, Brown carefully notes that autobiography is not the 'perfect genre' that it may seem. She explains that, to the extent that autobiographies may privilege certain generic plots (like the 'success story'), they may work to confirm a message that is opposed to the one which Brown thinks Grealy wants to tell. That is, Brown believes that Grealy's desire for 'wholeness' (whatever this entails) exists alongside her awareness of the impossibility of wholeness, so that her text deconstructs any notion of a 'whole subject', both deliberately and inevitably, in spite of itself. However, she undertakes this project within a form, which, historically, has helped to produce that subject. Autobiography may, therefore, provide the wholeness Grealy seeks, but only at the cost of denying the reality of her experience and simultaneously rendering it problematic as autobiography.

Brown's reading of Grealy's text is persuasive, but some further observations can be made. The desire for 'wholeness' Brown identifies in Grealy's text can be expressed in another way, enabling the autobiography to be read as a project of recovery. Grealy's desire appears to be to recover a self (possibly a pre-existing self, in the sense that Grealy locates her loss of wholeness entirely in relation to the onset of her cancer), which Grealy further understands as normative. Additionally, Grealy's autobiographical project is as much to do with gendered identity, as it is about illness or disability (it focuses more on the consequences of her surgery, than on the experience of being ill with cancer). Her desire for 'wholeness' also suggests that her text could be understood as engaging in a feminist project, scrutinising what Mary K. DeShazer identifies as 'five key ways in which women's ill bodies have been textually represented: "as *medicalized, leaky, amputated, prosthetic*, and *(not) dying*"' (2005: 13). Grealy's desire for 'wholeness', understood as a project of recovery, can also be considered alongside Nancy Miller's often-quoted observation about the contested relationship women (writers) may have with the consequences of postmodern and post-structuralist theories of identity:

> The postmodernist decision that the Author is Dead and the subject along with him does not [...] necessarily hold for women, and prematurely forecloses the question of agency for them. Because women have not had the same historical relation of identity to origin, institution, production that men have had, they have not, I think, (collectively) felt burdened by *too much* Self, Ego, Cogito, etc. Because the female subject has juridically been excluded from the polis, hence decentered, 'disoriginated,' deinstitutionalized, etc., her relation to integrity and textuality, desire and authority, displays structurally important differences from that universal position. (2002: 106)

Brown, too, questions how Grealy, whose body is inscribed with markers of gendered and physical difference, can write her way to wholeness within autobiography, which has historically privileged the white, male, able-bodied subject. Her autobiography's search for wholeness, though, does confirm Miller's sense that a version of identity and reality as verifiable and coherent may well need to be recovered. Another way of presenting the problem Miller outlines is revealed in Haverty Rugg's contention that anxiety surrounds what is perceived to be a 'denial of referentiality inherent in poststructuralist theories of autobiography, which consequently denies the subject the power of self-construction' (1997: 16). The difficulties which postmodern and post-structuralist theories pose for autobiography might be regarded as only the latest in a series of obstacles which make it difficult for certain individuals (those not white, male, able-bodied) to be recognised, described and represented as subjects. In that the history of autobiography continually tells the story of these struggles, it is ironic, complex, contradictory and impossible. It is punctuated by articulations of failure, and it refuses easy categorisation.

Mintz argues that Grealy's text 'reveals how thoroughly the equation between identity and an idealised definition of beauty can be internalised' (2007: 58). It is true that, particularly in the later sections of the autobiography, when Grealy is in her twenties and beyond, she appears to regard validation in the form of the approving male gaze as the ultimate legitimation of her own identity (Grealy 1994: 194). But she is also drawn to an identity as an 'outsider' (1994: 196), to a performance of androgyny as a means of enabling her to feel 'very far away from my own femininity' (1994: 203). She describes the sense of freedom she feels in gay clubs and notes that she gravitates to a group of transvestite friends in college (1994: 202–3). Grealy experiments with multiple performances of gendered identity, as part of a search for alternative models of self-representation and for a means of escape from the heterosexual economies of the male gaze and the idealised images it generates. While she registers her exclusion from dominant constructions of beauty, she ambivalently resists their pressures and struggles to relinquish her desire to match up to them.

The text's refusal of resolution is further complicated by Grealy's use of the face as literal and figurative marker of her identity. In both Armstrong and Grealy's texts, a particular body part metonymically designates the importance of gender to identity and the complexities of representing that identity. Hermione Lee argues that:

> Biographers try to make a coherent narrative out of missing documents as well as existing ones; a whole figure out of body parts. Some body parts, literally, get into the telling of the stories, in the form of legends, rumours or contested possessions. Body parts are conducive to myth-making; biographers, in turn, have to sort out the myths from the facts. There is a tremendous fascination with the bodily relics of famous people, and the stories of such relics have their roots in legends and miracles of saints which are the distant ancestors of biography. But they persist in a secular age, rather in the way that urban myths do, and are some of the 'things' that biographers have to deal with. (2005: 8)

While Lee's study focuses on biography and the lives of writers, in particular, her comments are no less useful for autobiography and, particularly, for autobiographies of illness and disability. Despite the obvious importance of the face in Grealy's text, her face (as image) is erased from the text, which includes no photographs, only those which come with information on the covers of various editions of the book, nicely illustrating that Grealy may be attempting to escape confrontation with the reality of her physical appearance by banishing signs of it to the periphery or even the 'outside' of the text. In another indication of her internalisation of her society's standards about female identity – a woman is not valuable if not attractive – Grealy claims that:

> This singularity of meaning – I *was* my face, I *was* ugliness – though sometimes unbearable, also offered a possible point of escape. It became the launching pad from which to lift off, the one immediately recognisable place to point to when asked what was wrong with my life. Everything led to it, everything receded from it – my face as personal vanishing point. (1994: 7)

To the extent that the autobiography suppresses Grealy's bodily identity, it suggests that it is, indeed, as Brown argues, autobiography which allows her an escape, however temporary, from her difference. But is that the same as wholeness? It is impossible to study Grealy's autobiography without recourse to Paul de Man's famous essay on autobiography, 'Autobiography as de-facement'. For de Man, autobiography can be understood in terms of its reliance on the rhetorical strategy of prosopopoeia, described as:

> the fiction of an apostrophe to an absent, deceased or voiceless entity, which posits the possibility of the latter's reply and confers upon it the power of speech. Voice assumes mouth, eye and finally face, a chain that is manifest in the etymology of the trope's name, *prosopon poien*, to confer a mask or a face (*prosopon*). Prosopopeia is the trope of autobiography, by which one's name [...] is made as intelligible and memorable as a face. Our topic deals with the giving and taking away of faces, with face and deface, *figure*, figuration and disfiguration. (1979: 926)

One way of reading de Man is to claim that any autobiography, however knowing and self-aware, attempts to present a coherent (whole?) self. 'Giving a face' explains the process of creating a coherent identity in autobiography. However, the act of 'giving a face' only functions to emphasise how the identity created in autobiography is a fiction, because the self constructed within its pages is reliant on language and signifiers. Autobiography testifies only to the fact that capturing the self truthfully in writing is impossible, so that autobiography de-faces its subject it purportedly represents, because the coherent self it represents may be a fiction and because the autobiographer is attempting to disguise this fact, by the process of 'giving a face'. Autobiography therefore forces the autobiographer to encounter him or herself as other, because the self created within the pages of the autobiography is not a truthful reflection of the author. If autobiography provides a means of 'giving a face', it may enable Grealy a means of creating an identity (that ideal face) she desires. However, this is de-facement, because it might represent an avoidance of the physical reality of Grealy's existence.

Grealy's text concludes with a scene in which Grealy sits in a café, in conversation with a man she has just met. Her location is unclear. She is in Europe, probably Berlin, with a small chance it could be in Scotland, where Grealy lived for three years during a period of surgery. That she is not in America may be indicative of her continuing difficulties in locating herself, finding a home. So far, America's promise has not been kept for her, and so she must go 'outside':

> I used to think truth was eternal, that once I *knew*, once I *saw*, it would be with me forever, a constant by which everything else could be measured. I know now that this isn't so, that most truths are inherently unretainable, that we have to work hard all our lives to remember the most basic things. Society is no help. It tells us again and again that we can most be ourselves by looking and acting like someone else, only to leave our original faces behind to turn into ghosts that will inevitably resent and haunt us. As I sat there in the café, it suddenly occurred to me that it is no mistake when sometimes in films and literature the dead know they are dead only after being offered that most irrefutable proof: they can no longer see themselves in the mirror.
>
> Feeling the warmth of the cup against my palm, I felt this small observation as a great revelation. I wanted to tell the man I was with about it, but he was involved in his own thoughts and I did not want to interrupt him, so instead I looked with curiosity at the window behind him, its night-silvered glass reflecting the entire café, to see if I could, now, recognise myself. (1994: 222–3)

Mintz argues that this scene 'stages a metaphorical looking away, as if to ensure that the text, and the identity narrated therein, remains open-ended' (2007: 68). At this point, it might be helpful to shift attention from de Man's emphasis on the act of giving a *face* as central to autobiography, to the act of *giving* a face. One of the central arguments of this textbook has been that it is useful to think of autobiography as often taking on the qualities of a gift. Here, Grealy thinks about offering the gift of her insight – 'it is no mistake when sometimes in films and literature the dead know they are dead only after being offered that most irrefutable proof: they can no longer see themselves in the mirror' – to the man with whom she sits, but she is uncertain about whether he will be receptive to it. As Mintz notes, it is unclear whether this attribution of disinterest, and Grealy's refusal to share her insight, reveals his genuine lack of care for her and Grealy's continued perception of herself as worthless in the eyes of men or something quite the opposite – her self-acceptance (she does not need his approval) (2007: 69). It is as if Grealy is developing de Man's argument, accepting that, like the self created in her autobiography, the ways she presents herself to others, or the ways in which they perceive her, are always fictions (like filmic and literary constructions). She apparently accepts this idea with equanimity, even excitement – 'I felt this small observation as a great revelation'. However, her comparison of herself to dead characters in fiction and film is chilling, suggesting that, to the extent her culture does not value or recognise her, she could be dead. More optimistically, if Grealy does not share her insight with her male companion, she *does* share it with her readers, from inside her text.

In an interview with Charlie Rose, Grealy claims that she has not written her autobiography to start a revolution and that hers is a solely personal journey. However, she also claims that her text is applicable to any situation in which a person is told: '"This is how reality works. This is how you work. This is how you work in relation to reality"'. Grealy argues that:

so many things don't offer us the space in which to say 'No, wait a minute'. We don't even necessarily have to know exactly what the answer to the 'no' is. But just the act of saying, 'No, I have a reservation about this, it might actually be something else', is an enormous step which very few people feel allowed to make, mostly because they don't have the language to do it. They don't possess the language of rhetoric in order to recognise when people are telling them something that's a label, like 'beautiful' or 'ugly'. Those are labels, they're not actual things.[3]

Many American autobiographies engage in acts of refusal, of 'saying no' to the inadequate ways in which their authors perceive the 'national promise' of democratic freedom and equality to be operating in their lives, in the societies in which they live. This gesture of refusal often takes the form of an act of self-presentation, which resists a particular 'label'. While these texts signal displeasure and anger, regarding the breaking of that national promise, they make promises of their own. This is because that act of saying 'no' creates the possibility of something like a loophole (lobe?) – a space from, or in, which to re-imagine ways in which that national promise may be kept. It is a space which often allows for and invites the possibility of strange, relational collaboration and reply ('"Come, we will have a profound evening"'). These promises, loopholes, are also gifts of sorts – they are confusing and unsettling, but they are full of (empty?) promise. Certainly, an autobiography may be a gift in a literal sense. The autobiography as text is a consumer object, so that it could partake of the conditions which render it impossible, in Derrida's terms, for it to be truly a gift (that is, a gift which calls itself a gift cannot be a gift, because it forces its recipient to offer something in return). Autobiographies may well function to show the impossibility of the gift – it is surely possible to read Franklin's offering of himself as a model 'to be imitated' as engaging in the circular process of 'specular recognition and self-approval', which marks, for Derrida, the impossibility of perceiving the gift as truly a gift (Derrida 1992: 23).

Indeed, in a recent article, Gilmore has expressed concern regarding a tendency in what she calls the 'neoconfessional brand' dominant in contemporary memoir, in which 'the preference for stories which can be unmoored from specific historical conditions to become "everybody's" story are currently edging out more disruptive narratives that take readers into the anxious realm of nonnormativity and the lack of clear moral guidelines they associate with culturally protected privacies' (2010: 674–5). This is a situation in which, arguably, autobiographies like Armstrong's would edge out autobiographies like Grealy's. However, perhaps Gilmore's concern is overstated. The threat of 'edging out' she describes is not new, but has always been present throughout the history of autobiography production in America. And as this textbook has shown, despite this threat, disruptive autobiographies have always been produced in American culture, existing in (vital, problematic) relation beside those which may threaten them, and which they threaten too (therefore, in every sense of Sedgwick's definition of 'beside', quoted in this introduction). And as this textbook hopefully demonstrates, autobiography may be understood as a gift which promises to refuse the impossible. Autobiography aspires to be 'truly a gift' by appearing as, presenting itself, as 'something else', some 'thing', some thing 'other' ... as an autobiography.

Notes

1. The journal *Biography* has recently devoted an issue (35.1, Winter 2012) to autobiography (and life narrative more widely) and the posthuman. See also Smith and Watson (2010), 167–8, 247–8, on digital life narrative.
2. Reading Armstrong as exemplary, an American success story, has recently become considerably more difficult, given that the truth-status of parts or all of this text may be subject to debate. The reading of the text offered in this chapter was made prior to recent revelations about Armstrong, and in good faith – a situation which provides an instance of the importance of the reader in reading autobiography, and an illustration of how the shifting nature of truth (and difficulties in determining truth) entail that readings of an autobiography (even, as in this extreme case, as autobiography at all) may be dependent on changes 'outside' the text.
3. Charlie Rose (1994), 'A conversation with Lucy Grealy', *Charlie Rose*, http://www.charlierose.com/view/interview/7201 (accessed 8 December 2011).

Bibliography

Adams, Henry ([1916] 2008), *The Education of Henry Adams*, Oxford: Oxford University Press.

Adams, Timothy Dow (1990), *Telling Lies in Modern American Autobiography*, Chapel Hill, NC: University of North Carolina Press.

Adams, Timothy Dow (2000), *Light Writing and Life Writing: Photography and Autobiography*, Chapel Hill, NC: University of North Carolina Press.

Anderson, Linda ([2001] 2011), *Autobiography*, 2nd edn, London: Routledge.

Armstrong, Lance (2001), *It's Not About the Bike: My Journey Back to Life*, London: Yellow Jersey Press.

Ashley, Kathleen M., Leigh Gilmore and Gerald Peters (eds) (1994), *Autobiography and Postmodernism*, Boston, MA: University of Massachusetts Press.

Austin, J. L. (1970), *How to Do Things With Words*, Oxford: Clarendon Press.

Bak, Hans and Hans Krabbendam (eds) (1998), *Writing Lives: American Biography and Autobiography*, Nashville, TN: VU University Press.

Baker, Jennifer Jordan (2000), 'Benjamin Franklin's *Autobiography* and the credibility of personality', *Early American Literature*, 35.3, 274–93.

Banes, Ruth A. (1982), 'The exemplary self: autobiography in eighteenth century America', *Biography*, 5.3, 226–39.

Banita, Georgiana (2010), '"Home squared": Barack Obama's transnational self-reliance', *Biography*, 33.1, 24–45.

Barros, Carolyn A. (1999), 'Getting modern: the autobiography of Alice B. Toklas', *Biography*, 22.2, 177–208.

Berlant, Lauren (1997), *The Queen of America Goes to Washington City: Essays on Sex and Citizenship*, Durham, NC: Duke University Press.

Bjorklund, Diane (1998), *Interpreting the Self: Two Hundred Years of American Autobiography*, Chicago, IL: University of Chicago Press.

Bové, Paul A. (1996), 'Giving thought to America: intellect and *The Education of Henry Adams*', *Critical Inquiry*, 23.1, 80–108.

Brooker, Ira (2004), 'Giving the game away: Thoreau's intellectual imperialism and the marketing of Walden Pond', *Midwest Quarterly*, 45.2, 137–54.

Brown, Sylvia A. (2006), 'Scripting wholeness in Lucy Grealy's *Autobiography of a Face*', *Criticism*, 48.3, 297–322.

Broyard, Anatole (1992), *Intoxicated by My Illness: And Other Writings on Life and Death*, New York, NY: Fawcett Columbine.

Burnham, Michelle (1993), 'The journey between: liminality and dialogism in Mary White Rowlandson's captivity narrative', *Early American Literature*, 28.1, 60–75.

Charlie Rose (1994), 'A conversation with Lucy Grealy', *Charlie Rose*, http://www.charlierose.com/view/interview/7201 (accessed 8 December 2011).

Couser, G. Thomas (1989), *Altered Egos: Authority in American Autobiography*, New York, NY: Oxford University Press.

Couser, G. Thomas (2009), *Signifying Bodies: Disability in Contemporary Life Writing*, Ann Arbor, MI: University of Michigan Press.

Couser, G. Thomas (2012), *Memoir: An Introduction*, Oxford: Oxford University Press.

Cox, James M. (1971), 'Autobiography and America', *Virginia Quarterly Review*, 47.2, 252–77.

Culley, Amy and Rebecca Styler (eds) (2011), 'Special issue: lives in relation', *Life Writing*, 8.3, 237–350.

Culley, Margo (1992), *American Women's Autobiography: Fea(s)ts of Memory*, Madison, WI: University of Wisconsin Press.

Cummings, Donald D. (ed.) (1990), *Approaches to Teaching Whitman's Leaves of Grass*, New York, NY: Modern Language Association of America.

Cummings, Donald D. (ed.) (2009), *A Companion to Walt Whitman*, Oxford: Blackwell.

Davidson, Cathy N. (2006/2007), 'Olaudah Equiano, written by himself', *Novel*, 40.1/2, 18–51.

Derrida, Jacques (1980), 'The law of genre', *Glyph*, 7.1, 202–29.

Derrida, Jacques (1992), *Given Time: I. Counterfeit Money*, Chicago, IL: University of Chicago Press.

Derrida, Jacques (1993), *Aporias*, trans. Thomas Dutoit, Stanford, CA: Stanford University Press.

de Man, Paul (1979), 'Autobiography as de-facement', *Modern Language Notes*, 94.5, 919–30.

DeShazer, Mary K. (2005), *Fractured Borders: Reading Women's Cancer Literature*, Ann Arbor, MI: University of Michigan Press.

Douglass, Frederick ([1845] 2009), *Narrative of the Life of Frederick Douglass*, Oxford: Oxford University Press.

Doyle, Laura (2009), 'Toward a philosophy of transnationalism', *Journal of Transnational Studies*, 1.1, 1–29.

Eakin, Paul John (ed.) (1989), *On Autobiography: Philippe Lejeune*, Minneapolis, MN: University of Minnesota Press.

Eakin, Paul John (ed.) (1991), *American Autobiography: Retrospect and Prospect*, Wisconsin, WI: University of Wisconsin Press.

Eakin, Paul John (1992), *Touching the World: Reference in Autobiography*, Princeton, NJ: Princeton University Press.

Eakin, Paul John (1999), *How Our Lives Become Stories: Making Selves*, Ithaca, NY: Cornell University Press.

Eakin, Paul John (2004), *The Ethics of Life Writing*, Ithaca, NY: Cornell University Press.

Eakin, Paul John (2008), *Living Autobiographically: How We Create Identity in Narrative*, Ithaca, NY: Cornell University Press.

Egan, Susanna (1999), *Mirror Talk: Genres of Crisis in Contemporary Autobiography*, Chapel Hill, NC: University of North Carolina Press.

Elmwood, Victoria (2004), '"Happy, happy ever after": the transformation of trauma between the generations in Art Spiegelman's *Maus: A Survivor's Tale*', *Biography*, 27.4, 691–720.

Equiano, Olaudah ([1789] 2003), *The Interesting Narrative and Other Writings*, London: Penguin.

Fabian, Ann (2000), *The Unvarnished Truth: Personal Narratives in Nineteenth Century America*, Berkeley, CA: University of California Press.

Fayre, Robert F. (ed.) (1992), *New Essays on Walden*, Cambridge: Cambridge University Press.

Firsch, Audrey (ed.) (2007), *The Cambridge Companion to the African American Slave Narrative*, Cambridge: Cambridge University Press.

Foley, Barbara (2009), 'Rhetoric and silence in Barack Obama's *Dreams From My Father*', *Cultural Logic*, 1, 1–46.

Frank, Arthur W. (1995), *The Wounded Storyteller: Body, Illness and Ethics*, Chicago, IL: University of Chicago Press.

Franklin, Benjamin ([1771–1790] 2008), *Autobiography and Other Writings*, Oxford: Oxford University Press.

Franzen, Jonathan (2010), *Freedom*, London: Fourth Estate.

Frey, James ([2003] 2004), *A Million Little Pieces*, London: John Murray.

Garfield, Deborah M. and Rafia Zafar (eds) (1996), *Harriet Jacobs and Incidents in the Life of a Slave Girl: New Critical Essays*, Cambridge: Cambridge University Press.

Gates, Henry Louis, Jr ([1997] 2004), *Thirteen Ways of Looking at a Black Man*, London: Vintage.

Giles, Paul (2003), 'Transnationalism and classic American literature', *PMLA*, 118.1, 62–77.

Gilmore, Leigh (1994), *Autobiographics: A Feminist Theory of Women's Self-Representation*, New York, NY: Cornell University Press.

Gilmore, Leigh (2001), *The Limits of Autobiography: Trauma and Testimony*,

New York, NY: Cornell University Press.

Gilmore, Leigh (2010), 'American Neoconfessional: Memoir, Self-Help, and Redemption on Oprah's Couch', *Biography*, 33.4, 567–679.

Gilmore, Leigh (2012), 'Agency Without Mastery: Chronic Pain and Posthuman Life Writing', *Biography*, 35.1, 83–98.

Grealy, Lucy (1994), *Autobiography of a Face*, New York, NY: HarperCollins.

Hawkins, Anne Hunsaker (1999), *Reconstructing Illness: Studies in Pathography*, 2nd edn, West Lafayette, IN: Purdue University Press.

Hejinian, Lyn (1987), *My Life*, Los Angeles, LA: Sun & Moon Press.

Henke, Suzette A. (2000), *Shattered Subjects: Trauma and Testimony in Women's Life Writing*, New York, NY: St Martin's Press.

Hirsch, Marianne (1997), *Family Frames: Photography, Narrative and Postmemory*, Cambridge, MA: Harvard University Press.

Huddart, David Paul (2008), *Postcolonial Theory and Autobiography*, New York, NY: Routledge.

Hungerford, Amy (2003), *The Holocaust of Texts: Genocide, Literature and Personification*, Chicago, IL: University of Chicago Press.

Jacobs, Harriet ([1861] 2000), *Incidents in the Life of a Slave Girl, Written by Herself*, New York, NY: Penguin.

Killingsworth, M. Jimmie (ed.) (2007), *The Cambridge Companion to Walt Whitman*, Cambridge: Cambridge University Press.

Kimmel, Michael S. (2006), *Manhood in America*, New York, NY: Oxford University Press.

King, Nicola (2000), *Memory, Narrative, Identity: Remembering the Self*, Edinburgh: Edinburgh University Press.

Kingston, Maxine Hong (1977), *The Woman Warrior*, London: Picador.

Lee, Hermione (2005), *Body Parts: Essays on Life Writing*, London: Chatto & Windus.

Lee, Maurice S. (ed.) (2009), *The Cambridge Companion to Frederick Douglass*, Cambridge: Cambridge University Press.

Lee, Robert A. (ed.) (1988), *First-Person Singular: Studies in American Autobiography*, New York, NY: St Martin's Press.

Linzie, Anna (2006), *The True Story of Alice B. Toklas: A Study of Three Autobiographies*, Iowa City, IA: University of Iowa Press.

Logan, Lisa (1993), 'Mary Rowlandson's captivity and the "Place of the woman subject"', *Early American Literature*, 28.1, 255–77.

Looby, Christopher (1986), '"The affairs of the revolution occasion'd the interruption": writing, revolution, deferral and conciliation in Franklin's *Autobiography*', *American Quarterly*, 38:1, 72–96.

Madsen, Deborah (1998), *American Exceptionalism*, Edinburgh: Edinburgh University Press.

Marcus, Laura (1994), *Auto/biographical Discourses: Criticism, Theory, Practice*, Manchester: Manchester University Press.

Meehan, Sean Ross (2008), *Mediating American Autobiography: Photography in Emerson, Thoreau, Douglass and Whitman*, Columbia, MO: University of Missouri Press.

Miller Budick, Emily (2001), 'Forced confessions: the case of Art Spiegelman's *Maus*', *Prooftexts*, 21.3, 379–98.

Miller, Nancy (2002), *But Enough About Me: Why We Read Other People's Lives*, New York, NY: Columbia University Press.

Mintz, Susannah B. (2007), *Unruly Bodies: Life Writing by Women with Disabilities*, Chapel Hill, NC: University of North Carolina Press.

Moore-Gilbert, Bart (2009), *Postcolonial Life-Writing: Culture, Politics and Self-Representation*, London: Routledge.

Myerson, Joel (ed.) (1995), *The Cambridge Companion to Henry David Thoreau*, Cambridge: Cambridge University Press.

Myerson, Joel (2000), *Transcendentalism: A Reader*, Oxford: Oxford University Press.

Nussbaum, Felicity (1989), *The Autobiographical Subject: Gender and Ideology in Eighteenth Century England*, Baltimore, MD: Johns Hopkins University Press.

Obama, Barack ([2004] 2007), *Dreams From My Father*, 2nd edn, Edinburgh: Canongate.

Obama, Barack (2008), *Change We Can Believe In: Barack Obama's Plan to Renew America's Promise*, Edinburgh: Canongate.

Olney, James (1984), 'I was born: slave narratives, their status as autobiography and literature', *Callaloo*, 20 (Winter), 46–73.

Oxford English Dictionary (OED), http://www.oed.com.

Parini, Jay (ed.) (1999), *The Norton Book of American Autobiography*, London: W. W. Norton.

Peters, Matthew (2005), 'Individual development and the American autobiography', *Philological Quarterly*, 84.2, 241–57.

Pipkin, James W. (2008), *Sporting Lives: Metaphor and Myth in American Sports Autobiographies*, Columbia, MO: University of Missouri Press.

Poetzsch, Markus (2008), 'Sounding Walden Pond: the depths and "double shadows" of Thoreau's autobiographical symbol', *American Transcendental Quarterly*, 22.2, 387–401.

Popkin, Jeremy D. (2005), *History, Historians, & Autobiography*, Chicago, IL: University of Chicago Press.

Potts, Laura (2000), *Ideologies of Breast Cancer: Feminist Perspectives*, Basingstoke: Macmillan.

Rifkind, Claudia (2008), 'Drawn from memory: comics artists and intergenerational auto/biography', *Canadian Revue of American Studies*, 38.3, 399–427.

Riley, Denise (2000), *The Words of Selves: Identification, Solidarity, Irony*, California, CA: Stanford University Press.

Rogers, Kim Lacy, Selma Leydesdorff and Graham Dawson (eds) (2004), *Trauma: Life Stories of Survivors*, Piscataway, NJ: Transaction Press.

Rowe, John Carlos (1996), *New Essays on the Education of Henry Adams*, Cambridge: Cambridge University Press.

Rowlandson, Mary ([1682] 2007), *Narrative of the Captivity and Restoration of Mrs. Mary Rowlansdon*, Sioux Falls, SD: NuVision Publications.

Royle, Nicholas (2003), *Jacques Derrida*, London: Routledge.

Rugg, Linda Haverty (1997), *Picturing Ourselves: Photography and Autobiography*, Chicago, IL: University of Chicago Press.

Sartwell, Crispin (1998), *Act Like You Know: African-American Autobiography and White Identity*, Chicago, IL: University of Chicago Press.

Sedgwick, Eve Kosofsky (1994), *Tendencies*, London: Routledge.

Sedgwick, Eve Kosofsky (2003), *Touching Feeling: Affect, Pedagogy, Performativity*, Durham, NC: Duke University Press.

Sekora, John (1987), 'Black message/white envelope: genre, authenticity, and authority in the antebellum slave narrative', *Callaloo*, 32 (Summer), 482–515.

Shea, Daniel, Jr. (1968), *Spiritual Autobiography in Early America*, Princeton, NJ: Princeton University Press.

Shulman, Alix Kates (1999), *A Good Enough Daughter*, New York, NY: Random House.

Shurr, William (1992), '"Now, God, stand up for bastards": reinterpreting Benjamin Franklin's *Autobiography*', *American Literature*, 64.3, 435–51.

Smith, Sidonie (1987), *A Poetics of Women's Autobiography*, Bloomington, IN: Indiana University Press.

Smith, Sidonie and Kay Schaeffer (2004), *Human Rights and Narrated Lives*, Basingstoke: Palgrave Macmillan.

Smith, Sidonie and Julia Watson (eds) (1996), *Getting a Life: Everyday Uses of Autobiography*, Minneapolis, MN: University of Minnesota Press.

Smith, Sidonie and Julia Watson (eds) (1998), *Women, Autobiography, Theory: A Reader*, Madison, WI: University of Wisconsin Press.

Smith, Sidonie and Julia Watson ([2001] 2010), *Reading Autobiography: A Guide for Interpreting Life Narratives*, 2nd edn, Minneapolis, MN: University of Minnesota Press.

Spiegelman, Art ([1996] 2003), *The Complete Maus*, London: Penguin.

Stacey, Jackie (1997), *Teratologies: A Cultural Study of Cancer*, London: Routledge.

Stein, Gertrude ([1933] 2001), *The Autobiography of Alice B. Toklas*, London: Penguin.

Strickland, Margot (1995), 'Ghosting an autobiography', *Biography*, 18.1, 65–8.

Stone, Arthur E. (ed.) (1981), *The American Autobiography: A Collection of Critical Essays*, Upper Saddle River, NJ: Prentice-Hall.

Swindells, Julia (ed.) (1995), *The Uses of Autobiography*, London: Taylor & Francis.

Taylor, Matthew A. (2009), 'The "Phantasmodesty" of Henry Adams', *Common Knowledge*, 15.3, 373–94.

Thoreau, Henry David ([1849] 1985), *A Week on the Concord and Merrimack Rivers*, New York, NY: Library of America.

Thoreau, Henry David ([1854] 2008), *Walden*, Oxford: Oxford University Press.

Tinnemeyer, Andrea (2006), *Identity Politics of the Captivity Narrative after 1848*, Lincoln, NE: University of Nebraska Press.

Todorov, Tzvetan (ed.) (1977), *French Literary Theory Today: A Reader*, Cambridge: Cambridge University Press.

Varner Gunn, Janet (1977), 'Autobiography and the narrative experience of temporality as depth', *Soundings*, 60, 194–209.

West, Andrew (2008), 'The education of Henry Adams: a bildungsroman', *South Central Review*, 25.2, 91–108.

Whitlock, Gillian (2006), 'Autographics: the seeing "I" of the comics', *Modern Fiction Studies*, 52.4, 965–82.

Whitman, Walt ([1855] 2009), *Leaves of Grass*, Oxford: Oxford World's Classics.

Wilkomirski, Binjamin ([1994] 1995), *Fragments: Memories of a Wartime Child-hood*, London: Picador.

Wong, Sau-Ling Cynthia (1999), *Maxine Hong Kingston's The Woman Warrior: A Casebook*, Oxford: Oxford University Press.

Yagoda, Ben (2010), *Memoir: A History*, New York, NY: Penguin.

Index

Adams, Henry, 15, 19, 21, 28, 31, 66, 85–94, 95, 96, 100
Anderson, Linda, 4, 13, 20, 22, 30, 104, 105, 108, 130
Armstrong, Lance, 22, 106, 127, 132, 136–42
autobiography
  and democracy, 8, 14, 30, 31–2, 44, 67, 79, 113, 126, 149–50
  and digital media, 130
  and Enlightenment, 8, 12, 15, 19, 20, 24, 30, 31, 49, 51, 63, 67, 103, 133, 142
  and gender, 4, 43, 52, 58, 67–9, 88, 92, 95, 128–9, 136
  and metonymy, 9, 68–9, 131
  and poetry, 4, 28, 79, 64–6; see also Hejinian, Lyn; Whitman, Walt
  and the posthuman, 130, 133
  and post-structural theories, 11, 12, 19, 22, 103, 104–6, 108, 111, 112, 129, 133, 145
  and readers, 5–7, 11, 17, 21, 50
  and representativeness, 16, 21, 44–5, 67, 68–70
  and truth, 10–12, 20, 21, 57–8, 65, 70, 104, 110, 111–13, 124, 126, 134–5
  as defacement see de Man, Paul
  as transnational, 10, 23, 30, 31, 52
  definitions and history of, 3–6, 7, 20, 30, 109–12

  ethical and political aims of, 16–18, 57

Berlant, Lauren, 8, 31–2, 43, 62, 113, 126

cancer narratives, 142, 145
captivity narrative, 33; see also Rowlandson, Mary
Couser, G. Thomas
  on autobiography and America, 19–20, 104
  on autobiography, memoir and life writing, 7, 11, 99
  on illness and disability, 131, 137, 144
  on reference, 104

de Man, Paul, 147–8, 149
Derrida, Jacques
  on aporia, 12
  on genre, 13, 135–6
  on gift, 17–18, 150
Douglass, Frederick, 10, 19, 20, 21, 28, 29, 31, 32, 52–7, 58, 59, 61, 63, 71, 80

Eakin, Paul John
  on ethics, 109, 112–13, 122
  on the relational, 10, 105–6, 108
Equiano, Olaudah, 20, 21, 29, 30, 46–51, 62, 63, 72

Series Editors: Simon Newman, Sir Denis Brogan Chair in American Studies at the University of Glasgow; and Carol R. Smith, Senior Lecturer in English and American Studies at the University of Winchester.

The British Association for American Studies (BAAS)

The British Association for American Studies was founded in 1955 to promote the study of the Unites States of America. It welcomes applications for membership from anyone interested in the history, society, government and politics, economics, geography, literature, creative arts, culture and thought of the USA.

The Association publishers a newsletter twice yearly, holds an annual national conference, supports regional branches and provides other membership services, including preferential subscription rates to the *Journal of American Studies*.

Membership enquiries may be addressed to the BAAS Secretary. For contact details visit our website: www.baas.ac.uk